YOUR INTRO

FILM·T.V.

COPYRIGHT, CONTRACTS AND OTHER

LAW

by
JOHNNY MINUS
and
WILLIAM STORM HALE
AUTHORS OF
"The Movie Industry Book"
x
7 Arts Press, Inc.

LIBEL
Contracts
Copyrights ©
Equipment Rental
Guilds & Unions
Forms
TAXES
Invasion of Privacy
F.C.C.
Obscenity
Glossary
Made Easy for You

This book is dedicated to **Andre F. Stojka,** Dean of the Cinema Department of Columbia College, to **Richard Bernstein,** who may or may not be a typical Hollywood film maker, and to **Leslie Kovacs,** who knew enough when his big break came.

"Every man who knows how to read has it in his power to magnify himself, to multiply the ways in which he exists, to make his life full, significant and interesting."

— *Aldous Huxley*

This publication is designed to provide accurate and authoritative information in regard to the subject matter covered. It is sold with the understanding that the publisher is not engaged in rendering legal, accounting or other professional service. If legal advice or other expert assistance is required, the services of a competent professional person should be sought. *—From a Declaration of Principles jointly adopted by a Committee of the American Bar Association and a Committee of Publishers and Associations.*

Cover and Illustrations by Donato Rico
Typography by M. Young (MARgraphics)

FILM – TV LAW

Manufactured in the U.S.A.

Library of Congress No.
Standard Book No. — 0911370-09-9

This is Volume 7 of The Entertainment Industry Series
For additional copies of this book, mail $10.00 in cash, check or money order to:
SEVEN ARTS PRESS, INC.
6605 Hollywood Boulevard, No. 215
Hollywood, CA 90028

INVITATION TO READERS

In this book you can learn about contracts, libel, invasion of privacy, copyright, law. You'll learn as much as this book contains, or as little as you want.

We use a variety of teaching devices — chapters, cartoons, contracts, forms, exercises. We tease you with forms which you can attack with pencils. You can cross out and substitute your own words whenever you wish.

You can gain a theoretical understanding of what you should consider in planning your moves + movies.

You will be able, by learning what is in this book, to save your lawyer much time he would otherwise need to teach you, enough to understand the vocabulary he uses and the basic law you can learn in this book.

This is important to us — we want you to understand that making movies requires legal knowledge, including:

1. Layman-level knowledge that the reader should have, because it is he who works so hard at his occupation in order to make movies.

2. Expert-level knowledge, because our society is complex and so is your life.

You are invited to read on.

William Storm Hale

Hollywood, California

iii

INTRODUCTION

The Bear said, "Call the book AVOID 101 LEGAL PROBLEMS. Filmmakers don't want to learn law; they just want to avoid legal problems."

The PRODUCTION MANAGEMENT — LAW class at Columbia College learned law (and loved it) as an essential part of their preparation for careers as employees, employers, and self-employed filmmakers.

This is the best book on law written by a college film class teacher and attorney specifically aimed at film students and aimed to help teachers of film courses. Naturally, film professionals who realize how important law is at every step of filmmaking from daydreaming to distribution, can make this book their written introduction to FILM — TV LAW.

There has long been a need for an introductory book on law aimed to help the filmmaker, so that he can AVOID LEGAL PROBLEMS.

This book meets the need.

It's up to you whether you want to increase your knowledge of law to increase your opportunities to work successfully in your chosen field.

This book was prepared by the same team which prepared THE MOVIE INDUSTRY BOOK, which is used by professionals and their attorneys to put together commercial motion pictures.

Walter E. Hurst

TABLE OF CONTENTS

CHAPTER 1

INTRODUCTION – THE CARROT
You Know Law.

You already know a lot of law.

You already know a lot of motion picture and television law.

Let us explore what you know while we attach identification and classification to your knowledge.

Criminal And Civil Law

You know that there are crimes such as murder, robbery, burglary, criminal libel, interfering with arrest, prostitution, obscenity. You know about criminal procedure such as police investigation, arrest, bail, prosecution, defense, examination, cross-examination, summation, jury verdict, appeal. This area of your knowledge can be classified as *CRIMINAL LAW*. In *CRIMINAL LAW* the court proceeding is started by a government (federal, state, municipal) against a defendant who, if convicted, may face jail or a fine.

You know about *CIVIL* litigation for breach of *CONTRACT*. The plaintiff (the party starting the lawsuit) alleges the existence of a contract, alleges the defendant did not live up to the provisions of the contract.

You know about *CIVIL* litigation which is not connected with contracts but is connected with a so-called *"WRONG"* (the technical word in law is *"TORT"*). The plaintiff alleges the defendant injured the plaintiff because the defendant said certain words to him (personal insult), or about him (defamation). Or, the plaintiff alleges the defendant hit plaintiff (battery), put the defendant in fear of being hit (assault). Or the plaintiff alleges the defendant hurt or destroyed plaintiff's car or house.

Thus, you already know some law and some classifications:

1. Criminal Law
2. Civil Law – Breach Of Contract
3. Civil Law – "Tort"

You are reading this book because you are interested in motion pictures and television.

You already know a lot of motion picture and television law.

You have heard about fabulous salaries paid to stars under *contracts* between studios and stars.

You have heard about *tax* law aspects of stars' contracts.

You have heard about high salaries paid to movie union personnel and about the power of motion picture unions (*labor law*).

You have heard about *copyright infringement, invasion of the right of privacy, libel* actions based on contents of motion pictures and television shows.

You have heard about the Federal Communications Commission (F.C.C.). There are numerous government regulations of business, labor etc. which apply to motion pictures and television.

You have heard about producers, directors, stars working for reduced salary and a "piece of the action." (*Corporation* law, *partnership* law.)

Criminal Law — Civil Law (Contract/Tort)

Let us place into the categories of *CRIMINAL LAW, CONTRACT LAW, TORT LAW* some of motion picture and television field law.

1. CRIMINAL LAW
   (a) Tax fraud
   (b) Criminal libel
   (c) Obscenity
   (d) Corporation Securities law violations
2. CIVIL LAW — CONTRACT
   (a) Producer—Star Employment Contract
   (b) Producer—Star Partnership
   (c) Producers' Group—Union Contract
   (d) Producer—Writer Employment Contract
   (e) Producer — Writer Copyright Assignment Contract

3. CIVIL LAW — TORT
    (a) Defamation (Slander, Libel)
    (b) Copyright Infringement
    (c) Invasion Of Right to Privacy

    (d) Invasion Of Right To
            Commercial Exploitation
    (e) Stock Fraud

You have been reading newspapers, magazines and books concerning law for years; you have seen dramatic trials on television and in theatres. You may have studied about law in the past.

You already know a lot of law.

Are you ready to learn more?

You have been buttered up during the last few pages by being told how much law you already know. You have been buttered up to buttress your faith in yourself and in your ability to learn more. You have been getting the *carrot*.

To make a donkey work, a donkey driver may use a *carrot*.

To make a donkey work, a donkey driver may use a *stick*.

Are you ready for a *stick*?

Reader — you *have* to know law.

CHAPTER 2

INTRODUCTION – THE STICK
You Have To Learn Law!

You have to learn law!

There is absolutely nobody who can help you *at the instant* you need your legal knowledge.

Let us explore whom you can theoretically ask for advice *after the instant* you first needed to know the law.

The first person you may think of giving you legal advice is an attorney. *Attorneys* are supposed to know some law.

General Practioners

Some attorneys are *general practitioners*. They can prepare simple sales of automobiles, can process simple incorporation procedures of simple corporations, can process simple estates and divorces for people with little property (some cash, clothing, car, residence). A lot of form contracts which attorneys prepare are prepared for both parties by the same attorney, are simple, don't lead to litigation. The general practitioner may know a little about various aspects of law. But over 95% of general practitioners know almost nothing about motion picture and television law.

Legal Field Specialists

Some attorneys are *specialists in various classifications of law*. Specialties include estate planning, taxation, probate, criminal, workmen's compensation, bankruptcy, corporate securities, real estate, creditors rights, selective service, labor law, copyright. Each of these specialists may assist motion picture and television personnel who *need help in the specialists' specific specialties*. However, the specialist may be unable to help supply sufficient legal information outside the specialist's specific specialty.

Economic Field Specialists

Some attorneys work within an *economic field*, such as the

4

industrial fields of (1) radio, (2) television, (3) motion pictures, (4) newspapers, (5) magazines, (6) popular music. These are separate and distinct fields. A (1) radio specialist may know almost nothing about (3) motion pictures. A (2) television specialist may know very little about (6) popular music. A motion picture theatre chain specialist may know very little about a motion picture producer's legal problems.

Movie Lawyers

The big motion picture studios thus have attorneys who specialize in the *industrial field* (motion pictures), *and then specialize in a field of law* (e.g. tax law, labor law, copyright law, trial law) *within the field.*

Most U.S. attorneys who have the knowledge required by you in your motion picture and television career practice in the *geographical areas* of New York City and Los Angeles County.

Most U.S. attorneys who have the knowledge required by you in your motion picture and television career are *very expensive.*

The least you can do once you have found an attorney right for you is to make your office conference time with your attorney as short as possible. If the attorney charges by the hour, the fewer hours for which you have to pay him, the *lower your bill* should be.

Movie Lawyer's Client's Knowledge

If you already have some *legal knowledge*, some knowledge of *legal relationships*, some *legal vocabulary*, then you will be able to organize your story better, and you will be able to understand better what the lawyer is talking about once he speaks.

In fact, if you have some legal knowledge which you apply in your daily work, then you may be able to *avoid* getting in some legal disputes in the first place.

If you are aware of when to see an attorney for a few hours to make sure that you stay within the law, *(preventative law)* then you may be able to avoid being on trial for weeks because you strayed outside the law.

Instant Legal Problems

The instant you require legal knowledge may occur at any time. *Situation No. 1* — The camera crew is slow in setting up cameras. You ask the property man to help move the cameras. Query — Are you breaking your contract with the *cameraman's union? Situation No. 2* — An extra brings her *11 year old daughter* on the set. You see the child, think of making your star appear lovable by having the little girl sit on his lap and say, "Tell me a story, Uncle Jim." Are you violating child *labor laws? Situation No. 3* — An electrician, during lunch hour at a desert location, decides to ride an actor's horse, is thrown and breaks his arm. Is he entitled to receive *workmen's compensation? Situation No. 4* — A sandstorm makes your automobile's windows useless. Are you protected by your *insurance contract?*

Each query shows the recognition of a legal problem. If the existence of a legal problem is recognized in time, then you can consider the possibility of avoiding the situation.

See the chapters dealing with: Situation No. 1 — Union Contracts, Situation No. 2 — U.S. Labor Laws; Child Labor Laws, Situation No. 3 — Workmen's Compensation, Situation No. 4 — Insurance.

Legal Forms

You can collect legal forms and legal form books.

Sometimes you may be able to quickly *close a deal* with a person who can't make up his mind by filling in a form contract the moment he agrees. Your firm may have a *standard contract* prepared for a legal situation (e.g. renting a house and surrounding land for the purpose of shooting a movie; hiring an actor for a specific day; option on a script; purchase of a script). If you know how to *fill in the blanks* (the other party's name, the identification of the subject matter, the amount of money, the appropriate dates), then you can do so swiftly whenever the need occurs.

Summary

To summarize:
You need *general legal* knowledge to *recognize legal*

situations in order to (a) avoid problems, (b) handle problems, (c) communicate intelligently with your attorney.

You need knowledge of law in your *industrial field* because (a) often no attorney knowledgeable in the field is immediately available, (b) you need knowledge to disqualify attorneys who show neither needed knowledge nor the training to perform swift and adequate research in the industrial field, (c) you wish to communicate swiftly with expensive knowledgeable attorneys, (d) the more you know, the better you will be able to spot and close good contractual relationships.

You need to know law in order to *better spot and avoid traps*. Some people consider certain persons in the motion picture and television fields as either (a) lions or (b) lambs. Lions kill victims. Lambs are eaten. You may save yourself from both the animal classifications of lions and lambs by having enough knowledge to remain civilized.

This has been the chapter of the big *stick*.

Do you want a *carrot*? Here it is. In this chapter you have learned a lot of law — the easy way.

CHAPTER 3

SOME CONTRACTUAL RELATIONSHIPS

(NOTE: The sample contracts in this chapter are designed for your education and not for actual use.)

Consider three (3) contractual relationships.
FIRST: Owner and User
SECOND: Seller and Buyer
THIRD: Employer and Employee
Let us apply these relationships to a theatrical costume warehouse and an actor.

Owner — User

FIRST: The OWNER of the costumes is the warehouse. The USER of a pirate costume on any specific day is the actor who rents the pirate costume.

Seller — Buyer

SECOND: The warehouse is willing to either rent out or sell costumes. An actor decides to buy a Western outfit. The warehouse is the SELLER; the actor is the BUYER.

Employer — Employee

THIRD: The warehouse decides to show its variety of costumes at a trade show. The warehouse employs the actor to model a mountain climber's outfit. The actor is employed for five hours at an hourly salary. The warehouse is the EMPLOYER. The Actor is the EMPLOYEE.

The three relationships are contractural relationships. The contracts may be written. The contracts may be oral.

Elements Of A Contract

The contracts may all have the following elements:

8

1. The parties.
2. The subject matter.
3. The consideration (a word you should learn).
4. The offer and acceptance.

Sample Learning Contracts

The FIRST contract may state:

OWNER — USER CONTRACT

1. The parties are the undersigned OWNER and USER.

2. USER is borrowing one pirate's costume on the following date: _ _____ and USER promises to return it no later than 10 A.M. on: _____.

3. USER promises to pay consideration at the rate of $10.00 per day for each day commencing: _____ until the day the costume is returned for the use of the costume. No rent need be paid for the day of return if the costume is returned before 10:00 A.M.

4. The parties agree to the terms of this contract.

OWNER _____ DATE _____
      Walter Warehouse

USER _____ DATE _____
      Alan Actor

The SECOND contract may state:

SELLER — BUYER CONTRACT

1. The parties are the undersigned SELLER and the undersigned BUYER.

2. SELLER hereby sells and BUYER hereby buys a Western costume delivered to and accepted by BUYER at this time.

3. BUYER hereby pays SELLER consideration of $75.00 as payment in full.

4. The parties agree to the terms of this contract.

SELLER _____
      Walter Warehouse

BUYER _____
      Alan Actor

The THIRD contract may state:

EMPLOYER — EMPLOYEE CONTRACT

1. The parties to this contract are the undersigned

EMPLOYER and the undersigned EMPLOYEE.

2. EMPLOYEE promises to work for EMPLOYER as a model, and to obey EMPLOYER's instructions, on December 14 of this year from 10:00 A.M. through 3:00 P.M. at the Tiffany Hotel, Main Ballroom.

3. EMPLOYER shall pay EMPLOYEE a gross salary (subject to withholding amounts for taxes) at $10.00 per hour for 5 hours.

4. The parties agree to the terms of this contract.

EMPLOYER: _____

Walter Warehouse

EMPLOYEE: _____

Alan Actor

Producer's Contractual Relationships

In motion pictures and television there are many contractual relationships. Some of these contractual relationships are:

1. Producer — Creator of original story.
2. Producer — Reader of stories and scripts submitted by writers
3. Producer — Scriptwriter
4. Producer — Producer's Secretary
5. Producer — Producer's Agent
6. Producer — Director
7. Producer — Stars
8. Producer — Actors, Actresses
9. Producer — Producers Guild
10. Producers — Organization of Producers which bargains with Unions
11. Organization of Producers which bargains with Unions — Unions + Guilds
12. A Union — Its Members
13. Producer — Cameraman
14. Producer — Etc.

You can look at contractural relations of a writer.

1. Writer — Typist
2. Writer — Co-Writer
3. Writer — Producer

Producer-Writer, 3 Relationships

The relationship of a Writer and a Producer could be:
      OWNER and USER
      SELLER and BUYER
      EMPLOYER and EMPLOYEE
The FIRST contract might state:
            OWNER-USER CONTRACT
1. The parties hereto are the undersigned OWNER (who is a WRITER) and the undersigned USER (who is a PRODUCER).

2. OWNER, who has written numerous stories concerning a fictitious lawyer named JOHNNY MINUS, and who is the owner of all rights in and concerning JOHNNY MINUS, hereby authorizes PRODUCER to use said JOHNNY MINUS in one feature film to be completed no later than one year from today.

3. PRODUCER hereby pays OWNER the sum of $5,000 today and promises to pay OWNER the further sum of $20,000 no later than one week before the first day of principal photography if OWNER does use the character in such a film.

4. The parties agree to the terms of this contract.

OWNER—WRITER:_____
                        Oley Wright
USER—PRODUCER: _____
                        Ustan Peters

The SECOND contract might state:
            SELLER-BUYER CONTRACT
1. The parties hereto are the undersigned SELLER (a WRITER) and the undersigned BUYER (a PRODUCER).

2. SELLER hereby assigns and sells and BUYER hereby buys any and all rights SELLER has in, to, or concerning the fictitious character, a lawyer named Johnny Minus.

3. BUYER hereby pays SELLER the sum of $20,000 and further promises to pay SELLER a royalty set forth in Attachment A to this contract, which is hereby incorporated herein.

4. The parties agree to the terms of this contract.

SELLER (WRITER) —_____
                        Sol Wroth
BUYER (PRODUCER) —_____
                        Ben Pren

The THIRD contract might state:

EMPLOYER-EMPLOYEE CONTRACT

1. The parties to this employment contract are the undersigned PRODUCER (EMPLOYER—FOR—HIRE) and the undersigned WRITER (EMPLOYEE—FOR—HIRE).

2. EMPLOYER employs EMPLOYEE as an employee-for-hire writer for a period of four weeks commencing November 1, 19——, employee to work on the premises of employer in an office to be furnished by employer, during the hours from 9:00 AM to noon, and 1:00 PM to 5:00 PM each weekday. Writer shall work on such projects as Producer may designate. All rights, including but not limited to copyright, in and concerning the work shall belong to PRODUCER as employer-for-hire.

3. The salary shall be $400.00 per week, payable weekly.

4. The parties agree to the terms of this contract.

PRODUCER, an EMPLOYER-FOR-HIRE

_____

Paul Hirer

WRITER, an EMPLOYEE-FOR-HIRE

_____

Whit Efh.

Summary

So far in this chapter you have learned that there are many different contracts, that key elements of each contract include parties, subject matter, consideration, willingness to agree, that in each contract the parties bear relationships to each other, that some of these relationships are Owner-User, Buyer-Seller, Employer-Employee.

Think

1. Who is the first person you saw this morning? What is your legal relationship to that person?

2. Who is the first person to whom you paid money today? What is your legal relationship to that person (or to his employer)? What did that person (or his employer) do for you (in other words, what was the subject matter of your contract)? How did you and the payee (party to whom money was paid) signify your intentions to enter into the contract?

3. Who was the first person to give you money? What is

your legal relationship? How much was the consideration?

There are many legal relationships. Some of these legal relationships are, and others are not, contractual relationships.

A contractual legal relationship may be governed by (1) the contract and (2) statutory law and (3) court made law and (4) constitution law.

Contracts. Classifications.

A contractual relationship may arise out of (1) an expressed agreement and/or (2) an implied agreement.

A contract may be (1) oral and/or (2) written, and/or (3) by conduct. Example of a contract by conduct: A blind newsdealer sets out his newspapers on the stand and in the middle of the stand has a cigar box containing coins. A customer takes a newspaper and drops the correct amount in coins into the box. the SELLER-BUYER contract is completed without any words.

In later chapters you will be able to read more about contractual and non-contractual legal relationships.

In later chapters you will be able to read about contracts which are longer than four (4) paragraphs.

In later chapters you will be able to read actual contracts used in the television and motion picture industries.

CHAPTER 4

CLASSIFICATIONS, TORTS, LAWSUITS
Elements Of Some Torts
Lawsuit Procedure

Law is like a seamless web, somebody has said and others have repeated.

Classifications

Attempts have been made to classify law into such neat classifications as:

1. Criminal Law
2. Contract Law
3. Tort Law
4. Constitutional Law
5. Copyright Law
6. Labor Law
7. Real Property Law
8. Law Of Sales
9. Law Of Agency
10. Family Law
11. Corporation Law
12. Law Of Evidence
    etc., etc., etc.

In Law School the law students may study about 24 neatly labeled courses bearing titles similar to the dozen named above, and bearing other titles such as:

13. Trusts
14. Wills
15. Bankruptcy
16. Labor Law
17. Personal Property
18. Creditors Rights
19. Patent Law
20. Probate
21. Common Law Pleading
22. Civil Procedure
23. Criminal Procedure

24. Administrative Law
        etc., etc., etc.

The same statute or case may pop up in several courses, in each of which another aspect of the statute or case is studied.

Let us continue exploring the concepts of legal relationships. In contract law the naming of the legal relationships helped to classify the contracting parties:

(1) Owner-User, (2) Buyer-Seller, (3) Employer-Employee.

Tort Relationships

Let us identify some of the legal relationship in the field of torts (civil wrongs).

THE VILLAIN	THE VICTIM
1. Accident causing driver	accident victim
2. Trespasser on property	property owner
3. Shoplifter	owner of merchandise
4. Insultor	insulted person
5. Person who hits	person who was hit
6. Slanderor	person who is slandered
7. Libeler	person who is libeled
8. Copyright infringer	copyright owner
9. Privacy invader	person whose privacy was invaded
10.Tortfeasor or (wrongdoer)	injured party
11. Defendant in court	plaintiff in court

You have been familiar with THE VILLAIN versus THE VICTIM since childhood. ("Mama, Joe hit me.")

You have also been familiar, that the self-proclaimed VICTIM may be a liar, at least according to the person accused of being THE VILLAIN. ("Mama, I did not hit Delia.")

You also are aware of the concept of defense. ("Mama, Delia is crying because she tried to hit me and when I moved away, she fell.")

You are also aware of the defense of admit a little and add more facts. ("Mama, Delia hit me and she hurt her fist on my face.")

You are also aware of the defense of justification. ("Mama, Delia hit me first.")

Concepts:

1. Wrongdoer and Victim.

2. Victim accuses alleged wrongdoer before the dispenser of justice (the court; Mama).

3. Wrongdoer can (a) deny Victim's allegations of wrongdoings, (b) admit some and deny some of the Victim's story, (c) add facts justifying the Wrongdoer's conduct.

Elements Of Some Torts

Let us examine some civil wrongs and definitions or elements of these civil wrongs (torts).

FRAUD

A complaint for damages for fraud and deceit should contain the following allegations:

(1) Defendant made a material representation of existing fact;

(2) That representation was false;

(3) Defendant knew the representation was false, or Defendant had no reasonable ground for believing the representation to be true;

(4) Defendant made the representation with intent to deceive and defraud plaintiff;

(5) Plaintiff's action that caused him the detriment for which he sues was taken in justifiable reliance on the representation;

(6) Plaintiff was thereby damaged in the manner and amount alleged.

NEGLIGENCE

To state a cause of action for negligence plaintiff must plead:

(1) Facts from which a duty of due care owing from defendant to plaintiff can be inferred by the court;

(2) An act or omission to act which constitutes a breach of the duty;

(3) Actual damage or injury;

(4) A causal relation (proximate or legal cause) between the defendant's breach of duty and the plaintiff's damage or injury.

PRIVACY

In stating a cause of action for invasion of privacy, the

complaint should include allegations of facts showing:

(1) Plaintiff's professional or personal status and other special facts tending to add to, or enhance, his general right to be let alone and not to have his name or likeness used or exhibited;

(2) Acts of the defendant constituting the invasion of plaintiff's rights;

(3) Injury to plaintiff proximately resulting from the invasion;

(4) Damages (in some cases damages are presumed to follow the injury);

(5) Absence of consent by plaintiff to the invasion (considered by many a matter of defense);

(6) Wilfulness or maliciousness of defendant's acts (where exemplary damages are sought);

(7) Inadequacy of legal remedy and irreparable injury (where injunctive relief is sought).

Lawsuit Procedure

The so-called VICTIM can file a lawsuit against the accused WRONGDOER. The person who starts a lawsuit is called a plaintiff. The other party, who has to defend himself is called a defendant. The pleading which the plaintiff files in court is called a COMPLAINT.

The defendant can, if he wishes:

(a) do absolutely nothing in court. After the defendant's time to plead has expired, the plaintiff can ask the court to award a judgment to plaintiff.

(b) file a DEMURRER in court. A demurrer states: Plaintiff's complaint is defective. It is defective for the following reason(s):_____. The court will have a hearing to decide whether the complaint is effective. If the complaint is defective, the court will probably allow the plaintiff to try to correct the complaint. If the court decides the complaint is not defective, the court will probably give the defendant time to file a pleading called an ANSWER.

(c) file an ANSWER. In the ANSWER the defendant can classify each paragraph (or sentence or clause if he so wishes) in the COMPLAINT as *admitted*, or as *denied*. Then the defendant can add AFFIRMATIVE DEFENSES. Then the defendant can counter-attack the plaintiff by alleging sufficient facts to show that the wrongdoer is plaintiff and the victim is defendant.

Plaintiff attacks.

Defendant (a) does nothing, or (b) demurs, or (c) defends and possibly counter-attacks.

This procedural sparring may go on for a while. The procedural sparring is (a) time consuming for the lawyers, (b) expensive for the lawyers, (c) expensive for the clients if the clients pay the lawyers.

But, this procedural sparring helps identify the legal issues, and may therefore shorten the trial, and thus save time and money for lawyers and clients.

The defendant may be able to win the procedural sparring and thus avoid having to go to trial.

The defendant may be forced to admit the correctness of the plaintiff's case during procedural sparring, may settle case, and thus both parties avoid having to go to trial.

During period before the trial each party can try to discover the facts known to the other side. These attempts may be made by *depositions* (examination by a lawyer of adverse parties and non-parties in a location selected by the lawyer, often the examining lawyer's office), by *interrogatories* (written questions sent to the opposition, which the opposition party is supposed to answer), by *examination* of the other party's documents, and in other ways.

Efforts to settle the case are made frequently during litigations. Often both sides have facts they want to hide, are afraid of the outcome of a trial, want to save the expense of a trial.

A trial is designed to:

(a) Allow the plaintiff to try to prove his case through the testimony of witnesses and the introduction of evidence.

(b) Allow the defendant to try to prove his case through the testimony of witnesses and the introduction of evidence.

(c) Allow each party's lawyer to argue for his side in order to convince the judge and jury.

(d) Allow each party to propose to the judge what the relevant law is. If there is a jury, the judge will instruct the jury in law. (How the jury is supposed to learn to understand the amount of law read to it in one long lump is a mystery.)

(e) Exhaust the parties emotionally and give them faith in the judge and jury so that each party accepts the outcome. (Possibly, this was a cynical sentence.)

(f) Determine and end the controversy. Sometimes the relief a loser feels concerning the termination of the tension caused by the legal battle is greater than his sorrow that he lost.

Theoretically, the loser can often ask for a new trial and/or appeal. Many losers do. Some losers win a new trial; some losers ("appellants") win the appeal. (The winners of trial court level are called "appellees.")

Summary

In this chapter we mentioned some classifications of courses of study in law school, which classifications also serve as convenient ways to discuss law in digestible lumps. We then took a series of tiny bites called "causes of action." We then set forth the elements of a cause of action; then we set forth the elements of another cause of action; then we set forth the elements of a few more causes of action. We hoped that you would jump to the conclusion that in each of the major classifications of law (criminal, contract, tort, etc.) there were lots of tiny bites (causes of action).

At that stage your reaction may have been: "There's too much to learn! Law is too complicated."

At that stage we brought you back to the familiar — basic civil procedure. You know the plaintiff files papers, the defendant files papers, the papers have children, and eventually there may be a trial. At the trial the plaintiff testifies, the defendant testifies, witnesses testify, evidence is introduced, lawyers argue, the judge and/or jury decide for one party or the other. (Of course the papers don't have children. It just seems that way.)

CHAPTER 5

COPYRIGHT
Introduction

The field of copyright law concerns artistic, literary and musical property and the right to commercially exploit such property by reproducing it in numerous ways.

You can argue with this definition and every other definition of copyright. Or you can accept the definition as an introductory statement.

The Copyright Office of the United States issues free forms and free circulars. You will be working with the forms to register your claims to copyright in scripts (Form C), songs (Form E), motion pictures (Form L-M) and other copyright protectible material (Forms A, B, etc.).

On the next few pages is a reproduction of Form L-M.

The circulars of the Copyright Office are written by knowledgeable people. Some of the circulars in vogue when this book was published are reprinted herein.

But forms and circulars are sometimes replaced by the Copyright Office. If you want to expand your knowledge about copyright, you can write for a copy of all free forms and free circulars to:

Copyright Office
Library of Congress
Washington, D.C. 20540

The following is oversimplified. Please learn the approach. But since there are unmentioned problems, consult with a copyright attorney before applying these general teachings to your project.

Let us try to apply copyright theory to motion pictures.

When the motion picture is completed, the copyright proprietor has common law compright in the picture. The duration of common law copyright is forever, unless it is terminated sooner. Common law copyright is terminated, by example, by "publication."

20

CLASSES	REGISTRATION NO.
L-M	DO NOT WRITE HERE LP LU MP MU

Application for Registration of a Claim to Copyright in a motion picture

Instructions: Make sure that all applicable spaces have been completed before you submit the form. The application must be **SIGNED** at line 10. For published works the application should not be submitted until after the date of publication given in line 5 (a), and should state the facts which existed on that date. For further information, see page 4.

Pages 1 and 2 should be typewritten or printed with pen and ink. Pages 3 and 4 should contain exactly the same information as pages 1 and 2, but may be carbon copies.

Mail all pages of the application to the Register of Copyrights, Library of Congress, Washington, D.C. 20540, together with:

(a) If unpublished, title and description, prints as described on page 4, and the registration fee of **$6**.

(b) If published, two complete copies, description, and the registration fee of **$6**.

Make your remittance payable to the Register of Copyrights.

1. Copyright Claimant(s) and Address(es): Give the name(s) and address(es) of the copyright owner(s). For published works the name(s) should ordinarily be the same as in the notice of copyright on the copies.

Name ---

Address --

Name ---

Address --

2. (a) Title: --

(Give the title of this particular motion picture as it appears on the copies)

(b) Series Title: ---

(If work is part of a series with a continuing title, also give series title)

3. (a) Nature of Work: (One of the following boxes **MUST** be checked. *For further information, see page 4.*)

☐ Photoplay   ☐ Motion picture other than a photoplay

21

(b) Description of Copies: _____ (Give running time, footage, or number of reels) _____

(c) Number of Prints Deposited: (For unpublished works only) _____

4. Author: Citizenship and domicile information must be given. Where a work is made for hire, the employer is the author. The citizenship of organizations formed under U.S. Federal or State law should be stated as U.S.A. If the copyright claim is based on new matter (see line 6) give information about the author of new matter.

Name _____ Citizenship _____ (Name of country)

Domiciled in U.S.A. Yes ☐ No ☐ Address _____

➤ NOTE: Leave all spaces of line 5 blank unless your work has been PUBLISHED. ◄

5. (a) Date of Publication: Give the complete date when copies of this particular work were first placed on sale, sold, or publicly distributed. The date when the motion picture was made or exhibited should not be confused with the date of publication. NOTE: The full date (month, day, and year) must be given.

_____ _____ _____
(Month) (Day) (Year)

(b) Place of Publication: Give the name of the country in which this particular motion picture was first published.

➤ NOTE: Leave all spaces of line 6 blank unless the instructions below apply to your work. ◄

6. Previous Registration or Publication: If a claim to copyright in any substantial part of this work was previously registered in the U.S. Copyright Office in unpublished form, or if a substantial part of the work was previously published anywhere, give requested information.

Was work previously registered? Yes _____ No _____ Date of registration _____ Registration number _____

Was work previously published? Yes _____ No _____ Date of publication _____ Registration number _____

Is there any substantial **NEW MATTER** in this version? Yes _____ No _____ If your answer is "Yes," give a brief general statement of the nature of the **NEW MATTER** in this version. (New matter may consist of compilation, abridgment, editorial revision, and the like, as well as additional cinematographic work.)

_____

Complete all applicable spaces on next page

EXAMINER

22

8. Name and address of person or organization to whom correspondence or refund, if any, should be sent:

Name _____ Address _____

9. Send certificate to:

(Type or print name and address)

Name _____

Address _____

_____
(Number and street)

_____
(City)   (State)   (ZIP code)

10. Certification:

(Application not acceptable unless signed)

I CERTIFY that the statements made by me in this application are correct to the best of my knowledge.

☞ _____
(Signature of copyright claimant or duly authorized agent)

Application Forms

Copies of the following forms will be supplied by the Copyright Office without charge upon request.

Class A   Form A—Published book manufactured in the United States of America.

Class A   { Form A–B Foreign—Book or periodical manufactured outside the United States of America (except works subject to
or B   the ad and interim provisions of the copyright law).
          { Form A–B Ad Interim—Book or periodical in the English language manufactured and first published outside the United
             States of America.

Class B   { Form B—Periodical manufactured in the United States of America.
          { Form BB—Contribution to a periodical manufactured in the United States of America.

Class C   Form C—Lecture or similar production prepared for oral delivery.

Class D   Form D—Dramatic or dramatico-musical composition.

23

Class E
{ Form E—Musical composition the author of which is a citizen or domiciliary of the United States of America or which was first published in the United States of America.
Form E Foreign—Musical composition the author of which is not a citizen or domiciliary of the United States of America and which was not first published in the United States of America.

Class F   Form F—Map.

Class G   Form G—Work of art or a model or design for a work of art.

Class H   Form H—Reproduction of a work of art.

Class I   Form I—Drawing or plastic work of a scientific or technical character.

Class J   Form J—Photograph.

Class K
{ Form K—Print or pictorial illustration.
Form KK—Print or label used for an article of merchandise.

Class L or M
{ Form L-M—Motion Picture.

Form R—Renewal copyright.

Form U—Notice of use of copyrighted music on mechanical instruments.

24

FOR COPYRIGHT OFFICE USE ONLY		
Application received	Prints received	One copy received
Two copies received		
Title and description received		
Fee received		
Renewal		

When to Use Form L–M. Form L–M is appropriate for unpublished and published motion pictures.

What Is a "Motion Picture"? The copyright law provides for two classes of motion pictures.

—*Photoplays* (Class L) include motion pictures that are dramatic in character and tell a connected story, such as feature films, filmed television plays, and animated cartoons.

—*Motion Pictures Other Than Photoplays* (Class M) include such films as newsreels, travelogues, promotional films, nature studies, and filmed television programs having no plot.

Unpublished Scenarios. The Copyright Office cannot make registration for an unpublished scenario, synopsis, format, or general description of a motion picture.

No "Blanket" Copyright. The general idea, outline, or title of a motion picture or of a filmed series cannot be copyrighted. Registration for a motion picture covers the copyrightable material in the film, but does not give any sort of "blanket" protection to the characters or situations portrayed, to future films in the series, or to the series as a whole.

Duration of Copyright. Statutory copyright begins on the date the work was first published, or, if the work was registered for copyright in unpublished form, copyright begins on the date of registration. In either case, copyright lasts for 28 years, and may be renewed for a second 28-year term.

Unpublished motion pictures

How to Register a Claim. To obtain copyright registration mail the following material to the Register of Copyrights, Library of Congress, Washington, D.C. 20540: (1) the title of the film; (2) a description (synopsis, press book, continuity, etc.); (3) for photoplays, one print (frame or blow-up) taken from each scene or act, and for other motion pictures, at least two prints taken from different sections of the film; (4) an application on Form L–M; and, (5) a fee of $6.

Procedure to Follow if Work Is Later Published. If the work is later reproduced in copies and published, it is necessary to make a second registration, following the procedure outlined below. To maintain copyright protection, all copies of the published work must contain a copyright notice in the required form and position.

Published motion pictures

What Is "Publication"? Publication, generally, means the sale, placing on sale, or public distribution of copies. In the case of a motion picture, it may also include distribution to film exchanges, film distributors, exhibitors, or broadcasters under a lease or similar arrangement.

How to Secure Copyright in a Published Motion Picture:

1. *Produce copies with the copyright notice.*
2. *Publish the work.*
3. *Register the copyright claim* by sending to the Copyright Office: (1) two complete copies of the best edition of the motion picture; (2) a description (synopsis, press book, continuity, etc.); (3) an application on Form L–M; and, (4) a fee of $6.

The Copyright Notice. In order to secure and maintain copyright protection for a published work, it is essential that all copies published in the United States contain the statutory copyright notice. For motion pictures this notice should appear on or near the title frame, and should consist of the word "Copyright," the abbreviation "Copr.," or the symbol ©, accompanied by the name of the copyright owner and the year date of publication. Example: © John Doe 1969. Use of the symbol © may result in securing copyright in countries which are parties to the Universal Copyright Convention.

NOTE: If copies are published without the required notice, the right to secure copyright is lost and cannot be restored.

Return of Deposit Copies. The deposit copies (i.e., reels) of published motion pictures are subject to retention by the Library of Congress. However, it may be possible to enter into a contract with the Librarian for the return of the copies under certain conditions, and contract forms may be obtained on request. Information regarding the contract may be obtained from the Exchange and Gift Division, Library of Congress, Washington, D.C. 20540.

Statutory copyright of published works commences upon publication with copyright notice. Statutory copyright for unpublished material commences with registration of the claim to copyright with the Copyright Office. Until 1949 the effective date of an unpublished registration was regarded by the Copyright Office as the date the copy was deposited. The initial statutory copyright period has a duration of 28 years.

During the 28th year, a registration of a claim for copyright for a Renewal period of 28 years may be filed.

Since 1962, Congress has passed laws extending the duration of renewal period copyright protection for one or more years at a time. Thus copyrights which had renewal periods expiring on and after September 19, 1962 are good until December 31, 1972 at the time of writing this paragraph on October 12, 1972. You will have to check current sources to learn if this pattern of extending the copyright renewal period was renewed beyond December 31, 1972.

To review durations of copyright protection:

1. Common law copyright. Forever unless sooner terminated by publication or other method.

2. Statutory copyright. Initial period, 28 years.

3. Statutory copyright. Renewal period, 28 years.

4. Statutory copyright. Extensions. More years.

Suppose you want to use a clip from any Charlie Chaplin (or Mable Normand, Fatty Arbuckle, Mary Pickford, Douglas Fairbanks, etc.) picture. You are willing to use any clip from any picture which you are allowed to use.

You may wish to learn which pictures are in the *public domain*.

1. Make a list of each picture in which the star appeared. Identify each movie on a separate index card in capital letters. On the next line, write your source of information concerning the picture by author, book, and page. That way you can go back to the source whenever you wish to. On the next line write information such as *year of initial distribution*, production company, distribution company, writer, director, co-stars.

2. Then see a *Copyright Office catalog* (available at some public libraries, law libraries, and the Copyright Office) which lists movies registered during the period covered by the index cards. Separate Copyright Office *cumulative* catalogs contain initial period registrations for 1894-1912, 1912-1939, 1940-1949, 1950-1959, 1960-1969. There are semi-annual

period catalogs since 1947. When you find a listing for a film in a catalog, then on a fresh line of the index card write down "Copyright Office Catalog. Cumulative. 1912-1939"(or other pertinent years). On the next line write all the information which appears in the catalog about the film.

It is possible that you don't find a listing in the Copyright Office Catalog for each film on each index card. Possibly (a) the film was *never registered* with the Copyright Office, or (b) the film was registered *under a different name* in the catalog in which you are looking or (c) the film was registered in another catalog (e.g. a film which you believe belongs in the 1940-1949 catalog was registered in 1939 and is in the 1912-1939 catalog.)

(a) If the film was never registered, and it was nationally released more than 28 years before your search date, it is *probably* in the public domain. We say *probably*, because some attorneys might argue that films are rented (not sold), exhibited (not published) and are still protected by common law copyright.

If a film is in the public domain, can you make a new film which copies the old film? Probably. We say *probably* because the old film may have been based on a book or other original work which is still protected by copyright, and some attorneys might argue that you are not allowed to copy the film because such a copy would infringe on the copyright of the original work.

If a film is in the public domain, and there is no other relevant copyright, can you photocopy that original film? Probably. We say *probably* because there are cases which distinguish between (a) the literary content as opposed to (b) the typography. A California judge, in a case, forbade photocopying the typography of a public domain work. A New York judge allowed the photocopying of typography in another case. There are cases which distinguish between (a) copyright in a song, (b) rights in a soundtrack. Permission to press records containing a song does not include permission to reproduce a sound track on which the song has been recorded. Thus, some attorneys might argue that a public domain photoplay may be copied in every way except by using the photoplay as recorded on a film to make more copies by chemical (film) or electric (videotape) means.

You may be upset by the repeated use of *probably* and some *attorneys might argue*. We are sorry about that.

3. The Copyright Office also registers applications to register claims to copyrights for Renewal periods. (An additional 28 years.) These Renewals are listed in different catalogs during different years.

In 1947 and 1948, the renewals by movies were listed in Copyright Office Catalogs, Third Series, Part 14A. Since then, Renewals for movies are listed in Copyright Office Catalogs, Third Series, Parts 12-13.

Renewals are supposed to be filed during the 28th year of the original copyright period. If the original copyright period commenced on May 1, 1915, the original period's 28th year commences 27 years after May 1, 1915: May 1, 1942, and ends April 30, 1943.

Thus, if your original copyright office registration was filed on May 1, 1915, you should search for the renewal in all catalogs which lsit such renewals from May 1, 1942 to April 1, 1943. At that time, 1942-1943, these catalogs were issued monthly. Search both all monthly catalogs listing registrations during those months (the registrations during any month appear in a catalog published months later). *Also* look at the annual indices for each year for listings of movies for which R forms have been filed. (*But*, you can't rely on these indices.)

Warning. The Copyright Office registrations of *published* works is necessarily after the publication of the works. The original copyright period commenced on the publication date of the work. The R form should have been (but not always is) filed during the 28th year after publication, not the 28th year after printed registration. But, the Copyright Office Catalog may not give you the original publication date. Therefore you *also* have to search Renewal catalogs for periods *preceding* and following the 28th year following initial registration of the work in the Copyright Office.

Unfortunately the Copyright Office Catalogs are not all perfect.

The Copyright Office keeps an index and on each copyright registration, concerning recorded assignments, and concerning other information. The Copyright Office renders services for *fees* to any interested party — such services include: (1) searching its files, (2) rendering reports in information it (a) found and (b) did not find.

After your preliminary searches (1) listing all movies, (2) searching for original registrations, (3) searching for renewal registrations, you may find possible public domain movies. You can then identify these movies to the Copyright Office, mention any original applications you found, mention any search for and failure to find an original original application or Renewal period application. Ask the Copyright Office to check their records and confirm whether or not the original and renewal applications you did not find was due to there being no such registrations.

You may wish to avoid all searching yourself and may simply ask the Copyright Office to search and report all original and renewal applications for all movies listed on a list you provide. There are three disadvantages: (1) The cost, (2) The longer time it takes the Copyright Office to prepare a lengthy search as opposed to a short search, (3) The lesser knowledge of the Copyright Office searcher who knows less about the films than you do.

Suppose your search of films of fictitious star Johnny Minus in books about Johnny Minus show his films include "Country Hero." When you or the Copyright Office search for a copyright registration of "Country Hero," no such registration is found. You (but not necessarily the Copyright Office searcher) look in the Copyright Office catalog under names of copyright claimants including Johnny Minus Productions, Inc. There you find no listing of "Country Hero," but you find a listing for "My Country Hero." You can then go back to your biographies and filmographies of Johnny Minus to see whether "Country Hero" and "My Country Hero" is/are the same film.

The above is fairly good as a general guide. But, there are so many variations that may apply and which are not covered here, that we must express our fear that you will limit your search to a do-it-yourself project, that you may do it badly, that you may be unaware of legal problems of which only an active copyright attorney may be aware.

At best, the above procedure *probably* applies to U.S. produced and released films shown theatrically. We are afraid to commit ourselves — because we (1) don't know all the copyright law which exists, (2) don't know what the future court decisions will be like. Foreign films are a different matter. The pertinent years and countries of original production or exhibition may be pertinent as to whether unregistered foreign films are in the public domain. Possibly a foreign film's visual part may be in the public domain, while the sub-titles or English language soundtrack is recorded by copyright.

Similarly, an American films visual parts may be in the public domain, while a later on added soundtrack may be protected by copyright.

*   *   *

What does all this mean to you?

You may have to make a film of a certain duration. You have to work within a certain budget. By dividing the budget by the length, you arrive at average cost per minute. You know that certain minutes will cost much more than the average amount. How can you compensate by having other minutes cost much less than the average amount? One way is to use public domain film. Can your characters spend time in front of a TV set or in a theatre while watching an old movie? Or, if you are shooting a documentary, can you use historical public domain footage as an introduction to your documentary, or throughout the documentary to contrast the old with the new?

You may want to copy scenes of a public domain film in a new film shot by you. Can you imagine your copying the famous steps sequence in *"Battleship Potemkin,"* also known as *"Potemkin"* in your first quickie horror picture, "Bullet Eating Babies Battle Teenage Baby Eating Barbarians."

If any reader ever makes *"Bullet Eating Babies Battle Teenage Baby Eating Barbarians"* and shoots scenes inspired by the steps sequences in *"Potemkin,"* please let us know!!!!!

CHAPTER 6

OBSCENITY, PORNOGRAPHY
No Predictions

A lawyer tries to serve his clients. The client who wants to stay within the law may present a plan to a lawyer and may then ask, "Is anything illegal?"

The client may want to raise money by interesting potential investors in purchasing stock in a corporation. The client requests for legal work, the lawyer can perform the legal work. The client asks, "Can I advertise for potential investors in a newspaper?" The lawyer can research the law and say "Yes" or say "No" or say "Yes, as long as you say the following: _____, and you avoid saying the following: _____.

The client may ask a copyright law question: "May I record the Nut Cracker Suite without securing the composer's permission?" The lawyer can apply the law and answer "Yes."

Obscenity Prosecutions

But, in the field of obscenity lawyers and clients are frustrated. There is no certainty whether a particular possibly obscene picture, gesture, scene, movie, (1) will cause people to be prosecuted somewhere in the United States, (2) cause defendant(s) to be convicted at trial level, (3) will cause the convicted defendant(s) to lose appeals.

Decisions which can cause trouble for persons connected with the creation, distribution, exhibition, sale of possibly obscene materials can be made by: (1) citizens, (2) organizations, (3) commercially minded persons and organizations who receive publicity and/or money to "fight pornography," (4) policemen, (5) prosecutors, (6) judges.

These troubles can be caused by these trouble-makers wherever in the United States these trouble-makers may exist.

The distinction must be made between (1) having trouble because a criminal breaks the law, (2) having trouble because trouble-makers want to cause trouble and use the charge that the law is being broken in order to make trouble.

In the field of obscenity, many persons are prejudiced. The persons herein conveniently labeled "trouble makers" are prejudiced against "pornographers."

The word "trouble makers" is not a neutral word. It seems to carry with the connotation that the labeler is prejudiced against the people he labels as "trouble makers."

Economic Warfare

The lawyer who advises his clients in the field of pornography must explain that so-called anti-pornographers wage economic warfare against so-called pornographers. The purpose of the economic warfare is to make pornography so expensive that the pronographer will cease participating in producing, distributing, exhibiting, selling pornography.

The trouble makers have seen so-called pornographers win in court again and again when the defense had attorneys qualified to defend pornography cases.

Therefore the strategy of many trouble makers is to cause economic loss by seizing films and merchandise, by causing disruptions through arrests and trials, by forcing so-called pornographers to pay high bail bonds fees and legal fees.

This long introduction is part of the living, breathing law concerning obscenity.

Many Obscenity Statutes and Court Decisions

The strictly legal part — the Constitution of the United States (freedom of speech); the constitution of the state in which the obscenity prosecution takes place; the various federal laws concerning customs, mail, interstate commerce; the various state laws concerning obscenity or causing the actors to violate sex laws concerning adultery, prostitution, exhibition, sodomy; the various court decisions, all are just background for the economic war fought by so-called "trouble makers" against so-called "pornographers."

Elements Of Obscenity

Before a work may be condemned as obscene, it "must be established that (a) the dominant theme of the material taken as

32

a whole appeals to a prurient interest in sex; (b) the material is patently offensive because it affronts contemporary community standards relating to the description or representation of sexual matters; and (c) the material is utterly without redeeming social value. . . . Each of the three federal constitutional criteria is to be applied independently; the social value of the books can neither be weighed against nor canceled by its prurient appeal or patent offensiveness . . ." The quote is from the case of MEMOIRS v. MASSACHUSETTS, 383 U.S. 413 (1966).

Fraud

It is also against the law to commercially exploit something as pornography when in truth it is not pornography.

The prosecution may have two inconsistent accounts. Count One: Defendant offered to sell a book called SEXXES I HAVE LOVED in a brochure which described the book as pornographic and therefore offered to sell pornography. Count Two: The defendant fraudulently represented a book called SEXXES I HAVE LOVED as pornography, when in truth and fact the book is not pornographic.

How can the defendant defend himself against both counts successfully? If he proves the book is pornography, the defendant loses on Count One. If he proves the book is not pornographic, he loses on Count Two. The defendant's only chance is to prove that the book may or may not be pornographic, and thus he can raise a reasonable doubt as to his guilt on either count.

Right To Read and Speak

The Supreme Court has held that a private person may read pornography, may possess pornography.

But the right of an individual to *read* pornography (which is legal) does not carry with it the right of a publisher to *supply* the reader with the pornographic book (which is illegal).

The right of a collector to collect pornography (which is legal) does not include the right to *trade* pornography with another collector (which is illegal).

How has the Supreme Court reconciled the First Amendment rights concerning free speech and the laws against obscene free speech? Very "neatly."

33

The Supreme Court Majority simply held that obscene free speech is not First Amendment protected free speech.

Waste Of Taxpayers' Money

The economic warfare commenced by "trouble makers" against "pornographers" has often badly hurt prosecutors and courts tied up by pornography cases. Many a court can collect over $50,000 in fines from hundreds of prostitutes, bookmakers, gamblers, marijuana possessors who plead guilty during the weeks which a well fought obscenity case takes. On $50,000 income a court can make a profit when it takes less than that to run the court. On a well fought pornography case, a court can make little income even upon conviction, and no income upon acquittal or eventual appeal court reversal of conviction. Do prosecutors and judges mind the economics of running their respective organizations? Some do.

Some prosecutors and judges enjoy publicity as "fearless fighters of obscenity," but dislike publicity as "dictatorial censors of First Amendment protected free speech."

Criminal Lawyer — Obscenity Specialist

In the field of pornography law, it is best to obtain the services of a criminal lawyer *specializing in pornography*, not just an ordinary top criminal lawyer. These specialists in pornography criminal law are very expensive.

Additional Factual Patterns

Factor patterns mentioned in some decisions concern: 1. Whether the material was forced upon the attention of unwilling recipients. 2. Whether the material was available (visible, purchasable) to children. 3. Whether or not the material was sold as pornography.

But the pattern of Supreme Court decisions are so mixed up, and the decisions depend so much on the prejudices of the individual members of the Court, that a lawyer cannot advise a client whether or not a motion picture with juicy scenes is or is not legally pornographic.

34

No Predictions

The mere fact that you have seen movies containing the same sexual action you wish to use in your picture, and the fact that none of the movies you saw were attacked as pornographic, does not mean that you will not be prosecuted for obscenity if you use such a scene.

Supreme Court Justice Black wrote, "My conclusion is that . . . no person, not even the most learned judge much less a layman, is capable of knowing in advance of an ultimate decision in his particular case by this court whether certain material comes within the area of "obscenity" as that term is confused by the Court today." Dissent in GINZBURG v. UNITED STATES 383 US 463 (1966).

CHAPTER 7

RAISING MONEY, CORPORATIONS
Single Proprietorship

A person may be in business by himself. This is called a single proprietorship.

Partnerships

A person may be in business with one or more other people. This is called a partnership.There are general partnerships and limited partnerships.

A limited partnership has two different classifications of partners: one or more general partners; one or more limited partners.

A general partner may provide services and/or money. A limited partner may not provide services and usually does provide money (or other consideration).

If the assets of the partnership are not sufficient to pay partnership debts, creditors can reach the assets of a general partner.

However, if the limited partner has paid in the full amount he promised to pay in to the limited partnership, and the limited partnership agreement has been duly filed wherever required by local law, and the limited partner has not forfeited his position as limited partner, then creditors of the partnership cannot reach the assets of the limited partner to pay partnership debts. (Of course, the limited partner, if he signs as co-maker of a promissory note or as guarantor for a partnership debt, can be forced to pay in his capacity as co-maker or guarantor.)

For income tax reasons, you *may* wish to raise money for your movie by starting a limited partnership.

Corporations

A corporation is born when papers called Articles Of Incorporation are filed in the appropriate government office (often called Secretary of State).

The persons who sign the Articles of Incorporation are called "incorporators."

The corporation tries to raise money by selling stock. The corporation gives a stock certificate to the stockholder, and the stockholder pays cash or other consideration to the corporation.

A corporation may have one or many stockholders.

A corporation may have a president, one or more vice presidents, a secretary, and a treasurer.

The stockholders have special and regular meetings (in theory or in fact). The stockholders elect the members of the board of directors.

The board of directors have special and regular meetings (in theory or in fact). The directors elect the officers: president, vice president, secretary, treasurer.

The same person(s) may be one or more or all of the following: incorporator, director, stockholder, officer.

Some American corporations have issued stock worth billions of dollars. Some corporations have sold $1000 or less in stock.

Theoretically, one advantage of corporations is that shareholders (who have fully paid in to the corporation the amount they subscribed for) are not liable for the debts of the corporation.

However, sometimes shareholders don't treat the corporation as a *separate* economic and judicial entity. Sometimes stockholders under-finance corporations. Sometimes directors don't bother seeing to it that corporations issue stock. Sometimes stockholders and directors meetings scheduled in the by-laws of the corporation are not held. Sometimes the corporation pays the personal bills of insiders or insiders use personal funds of corporations. There are other acts which should not be done, but are done by insiders.

In such cases a creditor of the corporation may sue both the corporation and individual stockholders. The creditor may argue, "Judge, if the stockholders don't treat the corporation properly, why should the stockholders be allowed to now prevent us from collecting money due to us from the stockholders? Judge, please give us a judgment against the stockholders personally." The court may grant such a judgment.

Therefore, it is very important for shareholders, directors, officers to honor the requirements of corporations.

Articles Of Incorporation

The Articles Of Incorporation state the name of the corporation, the specific purpose of the corporation, general purposes and powers of the corporation, the county in which the principal offices of the corporation will be located, the number of members of the board of directors, the names and addresses of the members of the initial board of directors proposed by the incorporators, the numbers and types of shares, and a few more facts. The incorporators sign the Articles of Incorporation.

By-Laws

The By-Laws of a corporation discuss *shareholders* (e.g., regular meetings, call for special meetings), *directors* (e.g., regular meetings, special meetings, action without meetings, number), *officers* (powers of president, vice-president, secretary, treasurer and other officers), *executive and other committees, corporate records and reports* (inspection of books, contracts — how executed), *certificates and transfer of shares* (certificates, lost or destroyed certificates, transfer on the books), *corporate seal, amendments to by-laws*.

First Meetings

The incorporators meet, elect directors, and end the meeting of the incorporators.

The directors meet, ratify the action of the incorporators in filing the articles, elect officers, adopt the corporate seal, authorize the president to notify the Corporation Commissioner that the corporation wants to issue stock. (Depending upon the facts and the stock involved, the Corporation Commissioner is either just *notified* that stock is or will be issued OR the Corporation Commissioner is asked for permission to issue stock.)

Securities Exchange Commission

In various circumstances (group them as "big time" for a quick oversimplification), the corporation needs permission from the United States' Securities Exchange Commission to issue stock.

How You May Be Involved

It is quite difficult for most people entering the television and motion picture industries to find jobs.

Many of the persons who have jobs in the motion picture and television industries do not keep these jobs for a long time.

Many jobs are for the duration of a motion picture, for the duration of a television series, for the duration of an industrial film or industrial film series, or even for shorter times.

Frequently both persons who are trying to generate jobs for themselves, and persons with more ambitious dreams, start production companies.

Companies require money, and money may come from backers. Backers may become general partners, limited partners, corporation shareholders, money lenders, credit lenders, etc.

A corporation may be able to sell small amounts of stock to numerous people and thus raise large amounts of money.

You may or may not *now* believe that you will become a corporate shareholder, director, or officer. You may innocently and ignorantly believe that you will not be mixed up in corporation entanglements because you have neither the desire nor business skill to become a corporation incorporator, shareholder, director or officer.

However, it is quite possible that a friend or business acquaintance who wants to start a corporation may ask you to be one of the incorporators, one of the directors, one of the officers because (a) he trusts you and (b) he thinks he can control you.

There are cynics in the movie business who state that the only persons they can really trust are their long deceased mothers. Some of these cynics trusted friends at whose request they helped to start corporations, or upon whose request they became directors or officers.

A director who ignores corporate affairs to the detriment of minority stockholders may find himself sued for negligence.

A treasurer who signs payroll checks may find himself liable to the Internal Revenue Service if income taxes withheld as payroll deductions from employees were not paid in to or for the Internal Revenue Service.

A president who signs major contracts without required consent of the board of directors or of the shareholders may find himself in trouble.

Thus, together with the corporate powers you have as incorporator, director, shareholder, officer, potential and actual issuer of stock, come serious responsibilities.

Money Raising Tools

A corporation is a tool. Properly used, it can serve the tool wielders and all who deal with it. Abused, the corporation can be used to hurt the insiders and outsiders.

The general partnership is a tool. Properly used . . . . Abused . . . .

The limited partnership is a tool. Properly used . . . . Abused . . . .

Tools may be simple or may be complex. The use of tools can be mastered by those so talented. Just as tools, so can corporations, general partnerships and limited partnerships be (a) simple, (b) complex, (c) mastered by those so talented.

CHAPTER 8

BORROWING AND BUYING EQUIPMENT

Borrow Or Buy?

1. Should you borrow or buy equipment such as motion picture, still and video cameras; dollies; light meters; lights, cables, tape recorders; microphones; woodworking tools; etc.?

2. There is no simple answer.

3. Some producers want to use services of a cameraman who owns his own motion picture equipment; the package of man-and-machine may be cheaper and much more reliable than the alternative of hiring a man to run specific machines (cameras) whose quirks are not known to the machine operator (the cameraman).

4. Many union comeramen are paid union scale because the employer and the employee are both *afraid to violate union rules;* such cameramen may sweeten their cost to the producer by contributing the use of their cameras.

5. Thus, owning a camera may be a way of *buying a job* — if you are hired. If you are not yet competent, owning a camera and studying it and its use dilligently *may* make you competent.

6. One of the problems with owning a specific piece of equipment, is that you may not have the *right equipment for the job*. If you own a 35mm motion picture camera, and you are hired to shoot a 16mm camera, you will have to borrow or rent a 16mm camera.

7. Another problem with buying equipment, is the *possible misuse* of available cash or credit to buy the camera. You may use up cash or credit you could have spent to make a movie (which now, that you have used up your funds, you don't have enough money to shoot). Or you may be much better off owning the camera than making a movie.

Contracts, Legal Relationships

Have you trained yourself to see the legal relations and contracts in the above paragraphs?

Paragraph 1: Lessor — Lessee, Seller — Buyer.

Paragraph 3: Employer/lessee — Employee/lessor or two independent contractors.

Paragraph 4: Employer-Employee, Employer-Union, Employee-Union.

Paragraph 6: Producer's employee is lessee of camera store's property.

Paragraph 7: Seller/creditor — Buyer/debtor.

The contract, concerning equipment sale or rental between a camera store and a buyer/lessee/user who leases the equipment from the lessor-store, is generally selected by the store. The contract front page often contains the names of the *parties*, the identification of the *equipment*, the rental *dollar amount*, the relevant *dates*. The back of the contract contains the *"small print"* provisions which favor the store over the camera user, especially if anything is or goes wrong with the equipment.

Small Print

The next few pages contain "small print" similar to that used by some motion picture equipment rental houses on their contracts.

Please read each paragraph, consider what problems are anticipated by the equipment user, consider what you should do to protect yourself.

There are some laws which *in some cases*, depending on the facts, *may* offer some assistance to camera users who find themselves at the short end of this contract.

LESSOR-OWNER MOTION PICTURE SERVICES
Hollywood, California

rental order #

Prepared by	Taken out	Rent status	Due back	Returned	Chckd. in by	Days Rt.
	date a.m. p.m.			date a.m p.m		

Rented to: _____ Deliver to: _____

_____ _____

_____ _____

Ordered by _____ Terms __ Open account (OK by _____)

__ C.O.D.

Order No. _____ Phone _____ __ Deposit (Amt. $ _____)

Out	In	Quan	Description	Price day/wk.	Amount	Total
			Accepted for return			
			Subject to count & inspection			

**LESSEE IS RESPONSIBLE FOR INSURANCE ON ALL EQUIPMENT
(SEE REVERSE OF THIS ORDER).
SIGNATURE CERTIFIES AGREEMENT TO TERMS OF CONTRACT ON
REVERSE OF THIS FORM**

COMPANY NAME _____

YOUR NAME _____ **DATE** _____

LESSOR-OWNER MOTION PICTURE SERVICES
HEREINAFTER CALLED LESSOR OR OWNER

1. IT IS AGREED THAT THE CUSTOMER-LESSEE AND/OR PURCHASER, HEREIN CALLED LESSEE, WILL TEST THE CAMERA(S) AND/OR OTHER EQUIPMENT HEREWITH SOLD OR RENTED, WITHIN 48 HOURS FROM THIS DATE AND PRIOR TO UTILIZING THE SAME FOR ANY PURPOSE AND IN THE EVENT THE SAME IS NOT IN GOOD WORKING ORDER, LESSEE AND/OR PURCHASER AGREES TO FORTHWITH RETURN THE SAID CAMERA OR CAMERAS AND/OR EQUIPMENT FOR REPLACEMENT OR REPAIR. UPON FAILURE TO RETURN SAID CAMERA(S) AND/OR EQUIPMENT THEN IT IS AGREED THAT THEREAFTER ALL DEFECTS DISCOVERED AS RESULTING DURING THE USE OF THE CAMERA(S) AND/OR EQUIPMENT WHILE IN THE POSSESSION CUSTODY OR UNDER THE CONTROL OF THE LESSEE AND/OR PURCHASER, ARE THE SOLE RESPONSIBILITY OF THE LESSEE AND/OR PURCHASER WHO ASSUMES THE SOLE AND EXCLUSIVE LIABILITY FOR THE CONSEQUENCES RESULTING FROM THE USE OF THE CAMERA OR CAMERAS AND/OR EQUIPMENT AND IN ADDITION LIABILITY FOR THE DAMAGE TO THE CAMERA(S) AND/OR EQUIPMENT OF THE SAME IS UNDER LEASE. ANY DEFECTS HEREIN REFERRED TO SHALL APPLY WHETHER THE SAME ARE LATENT OR PATENT. IN THE CASE OF CAMERA(S) AND/OR EQUIPMENT PURCHASED, THE PARTIES AGREE THAT THE SELLER MAKES

NO WARRANTIES WITH RESPECT TO THE SAME EITHER EXPRESS OR IMPLIED. IN THE CASE OF RENTED CAMERA(S) AND/OR EQUIPMENT THE LESSEE EXCLUSIVELY ASSUMES ALL RESPONSIBILITY FOR INJURIES TO PERSON OR PROPERTY INCLUDING BUT NOT LIMITED TO FILMED SEQUENCES AND ALL COSTS INCURRED IN OBTAINING SAME, RESULTING FROM OR ATTRIBUTABLE TO SAID CAMERA(S) AND/OR EQUIPMENT, WITHOUT LIMITATION OR RESTRICTION AND WHETHER RESULTING FROM OR ARISING OUT OF NEGLIGENCE ON BREACH OF WARRANTY ON PART OF THE OWNER. LESSEE AGREES IT WILL NOT SUB-LET CAMERA(S) AND/OR EQUIPMENT WITHOUT THE WRITTEN CONSENT OF LESSOR. THIS PARAGRAPH SHALL BE APPLICABLE TO ALL FUTURE RENTALS BY LESSEE FROM LESSOR WHETHER SIGNED FOR OR NOT, LESSEE AGREEING THAT THE TERMS OF THIS PARAGRAPH SHALL ALWAYS BE IN EFFECT IN LESSEE'S FUTURE DEALINGS WITH LESSOR.

2. THE LESSEE SHALL, AT HIS OWN COST AND EXPENSE, DURING THE TERM OF RENTAL, KEEP AND MAINTAIN, IN HIS OWN CUSTODY AT THE AFORESAID ADDRESS, THE SAID CAMERA(S) AND/OR EQUIPMENT IN GOOD STATE OF CONDITION AND REPAIR, REASONABLE WEAR AND TEAR ACCEPTED, AND SHALL AT THE TERMINATION OF THE RENTAL REPLACE SUCH OF THE SAID CAMERA AND/OR CAMERA EQUIPMENT AS MAY BE LOST, STOLEN OR MISSING OR BROKEN OR DAMAGED, OTHERWISE THAN BY REASONABLE WEAR AND TEAR, BY OTHERS OF A SIMILAR NATURE AND OF EQUAL VALUE OR SHALL PAY TO THE OWNER COMPENSATION ON ACCOUNT OF ANY OF THE SAID ARTICLES WHICH MAY BE LOST, STOLEN OR MISSING OR BROKEN OR DAMAGED.

3. THE LESSEE FURTHER AGREES TO BE AN INSURER OF THE CAMERA AND/OR EQUIPMENT FOR THE PERIOD THAT THE CAMERA AND/OR EQUIPMENT ARE AWAY FROM THE PREMISES OF LESSOR AGAINST ANY LOSS WHATSOEVER AND TO ASSUME FULL RESPONSIBILITY FOR THE CAMERA AND ALL EQUIPMENT RENTED, AND ALSO AGREES TO COMPENSATE LESSOR TO THE FULL VALUE SHOULD SAID CAMERA AND/OR EQUIPMENT BE LOST, STOLEN OR MISSING OR BROKEN OR DAMAGED BY ANY CAUSE WHATSOEVER, WHETHER DUE TO LESSEE'S FAULT OR NOT. THE LESSEE FURTHER AGREES TO COMPENSATE THE OWNER IN RENT FOR ANY TIME LOST AS A RESULT OF REPLACEMENT OF THE NECESSITY FOR MAKING REPAIRS ON SAID CAMERA AND/OR EQUIPMENT LOST, STOLEN OR MISSING OR BROKEN OR DAMAGED OTHERWISE THAN AS A RESULT OF THE REASONABLE WEAR AND TEAR.

4. THE LESSEE FURTHER AGREES THAT THE LEASED PROPERTY DESCRIBED HEREIN WILL NOT BE TAKEN FROM THE GROUND IN AN AIRPLANE OR ANY MACHINE USED FOR AIR TRAVEL EITHER LIGHTER OR HEAVIER THAN AIR, WITHOUT WRITTEN CONSENT OF THE OWNER FIRST OBTAINED.

5. THE LESSEE SHALL NOT REMOVE ANY EQUIPMENT FROM THE ADDRESS HEREINABOVE SET FORTH, WITHOUT FIRST HAVING NOTIFIED LESSOR AND FIRST OBTAINED FROM IT A CONSENT IN WRITING FOR SUCH REMOVAL THEREFROM.

6. THE CAMERA AND/OR EQUIPMENT HEREIN SHALL BE DELIVERED AND RETURNED BY THE LESSEE AT HIS OWN RISK, COST, AND EXPENSE. RENTAL OF ALL EQUIPMENT TAKEN OUT MUST BE PAID FOR THE PERIOD OF TIME UNTIL IT IS RETURNED TO LESSOR. NO ALLOWANCE WILL BE

MADE FOR THE REASON THAT ANY PART OF IT WAS NOT USED.

7. THE LESSEE SHALL, AT HIS OWN COST AND EXPENSE, BUT FOR THE BENEFIT OF LESSOR, IMMEDIATELY INSURE THE SAID EQUIPMENT FOR THE FULL VALUE AGAINST LOSS, OR DAMAGE BY FIRE, THEFT, WATER, OR ACT OF GOD, IN A QUALIFIED, REPUTABLE INSURANCE COMPANY AND SHALL DELIVER THE SAID INSURANCE POLICY TO LESSOR TOGETHER WITH THE RECEIPT FOR PREMIUMS THEREUNDER. IF LESSOR, BY REASON OF SUCH INSURANCE AGAINST LOSS BY FIRE, THEFT, WATER, OR ACT OF GOD, SHALL RECEIVE ANY SUM OR SUMS OF MONEY, SUCH AMOUNT MAY BE RETAINED AND APPLIED BY IT TOWARDS THE REPAIR OR REPLACEMENT OF THE SAID CAMERA AND/OR EQUIPMENT, OR IT MAY REMOVE THE DAMAGED CAMERA AND/OR EQUIPMENT AND, IN LIEU THEREOF, SUBSTITUTE A NEW CAMERA AND/OR EQUIPMENT OF LIKE KIND AND QUALITY, AND ANY SUCH CAMERA AND/OR EQUIPMENT, WHETHER REPAIRED OR SUBSTITUTED, SHALL BE SUBJECT TO ALL THE TERMS AND CONDITIONS HEREIN.

8. IT SHALL BE LAWFUL FOR THE OWNER OR ITS AGENTS AT ALL REASONABLE TIMES TO ENTER THE PREMISES UPON WHICH SAID CAMERA AND/OR EQUIPMENT IS KEPT FOR THE PURPOSE OF VIEWING THE STATE AND CONDITION OF SAID CAMERA AND/OR EQUIPMENT.

9. IF THE LESSEE SHALL DEFAULT ON ANY OF THE TERMS, COVENANTS AND CONDITIONS HEREIN, OR IN PUNCTUALLY MAKING ANY OF THE PAYMENTS AFORESAID, OR IF ANY EXECUTION OR OTHER UNIT OR PROCESS SHALL BE ISSUED IN ANY ACTION OR PROCEEDING AGAINST THE LESSEE, WHEREBY THE SAID EQUIPMENT MAY BE SEIZED OR TAKEN OR DISTRAINED, OR IF A PROCEEDING IN BANKRUPCY, RECEIVERSHIP, OR INSOLVENCY SHALL BE INSTITUTED BY OR AGAINST THE LESSEE OR HIS PROPERTY, OR IF THE LESSEE SHALL ENTER INTO ANY ARRANGEMENT OR COMPOSITION WITH HIS CREDITORS, OR IN THE EVENTTHAT ANY JUDGMENT IS OBTAINED AGAINST THE LESSEE, THEN AND IN ANY SUCH EVENT, LESSOR SHALL HAVE THE OPTION TO RETAKE IMMEDIATE POSSESSION OF SAID EQUIPMENT AND, FOR SUCH PURPOSE LESSOR, ITS AGENTS OR EMPLOYEES MAY ENTER UPON ANY PREMISES WHERE SAID EQUIPMENT MAY BE, AND MAY REMOVE THE SAME THEREFROM, WITH OR WITHOUT FORCE AND WITH OR WITHOUT NOTICE OF INTENTION TO RETAKE THE SAME, WITHOUT BEING LIABLE TO ANY SUIT OR ACTION OR OTHER PROCEEDING BY THE LESSEE.

10. UPON THE LESSOR RETAKING POSSESSION OF THE SAID EQUIPMENT PURSUANT TO THE PROVISIONS OF THE PRECEDING ARTICLE HEREOF, THIS AGREEMENT SHALL THENCEFORTH TERMINATE, WITHOUT PREJUDICE TO ANY RIGHT OR CLAIM FOR ARREARS OF RENT, IF ANY, OR ON ACCOUNT OF ANY PRECEDING BREACH OR BREACHES OF THIS AGREEMENT, OR THE LOS OF RENTAL FOR THE BALANCE OF THE UNEXPIRED TERM HEREIN, OR FOR ANY OTHER CLAIM THAT LESSOR MAY HAVE AGAINST LESSEE.

11. THE LESSEE SHALL NOT SUB-LEASE THE SAID EQUIPMENT OR LOAN THE SAME TO ANY OTHER PERSON, FIRM OR CORPORATION, AND SAID EQUIPMENT SHALL AT ALL TIMES REMAIN UNDER IMMEDIATE CONTROL, SUPERVISION AND DIRECTION OF THE LESSEE PERSONALLY.

12. THE LESSEE AGREES NOT TO REMOVE THE TAG OR NAME PLATE ON

THE EQUIPMENT SHOWING OWNERSHIP IN LESSOR.

13. THE LESSEE DOES HEREBY GRANT TO LESSOR AN OPTION TO TERMINATE THIS AGREEMENT ON 24 HOURS WRITTEN NOTICE BY REGISTERED MAIL OR PERSONAL SERVICE. ON THE OCCURRENCE OF SAID EVENT, THE LESSEE SHALL IMMEDIATELY RETURN TO LESSOR, AT THE LESSEE'S RISK AND EXPENSE, THE CAMERA AND/OR EQUIPMENT, IN THE SAME CONDITION AS WHEN FIRST RENTED, AND LESSOR SHALL THEREUPON, UPON SAID RECEIPT, REFUND THE UNEXPIRED PORTION OF THE RENTAL.

14. THE LESSEE AGREES TO PAY ALL REASONABLE ATTORNEY'S FEES AND COSTS INCURRED BY LESSOR IN PROTECTING ITS RIGHTS OR PROPERTY UNDER THIS AGREEMENT, OR IN SUING THE LESSEE FOR A BREACH OF THIS AGREEMENT.

15. THE ACCEPTANCE OF THE RETURN OF THE RENTED CAMERA AND/OR EQUIPMENT IS NOT A WAIVER BY LESSOR OF ANY CLAIMS THAT IT MAY HAVE AGAINST THE LESSEE, NOR A WAIVER OF CLAIMS FOR LATENT OR PATENT DAMAGE TO THE CAMERA AND/OR EQUIPMENT.

16. THIS AGREEMENT CONTAINS THE ENTIRE UNDERSTANDING BETWEEN THE PARTIES, INCLUDING REPRESENTATIONS, AND MAY NOT BE MODIFIED EXCEPT BY ANOTHER AGREEMENT IN WRITING SIGNED BY BOTH PARTIES TO THIS AGREEMENT.

17. NO TERMS, REPRESENTATIONS OR WARRANTY, EXPRESS OR IMPLIED, NOT HEREIN SET FORTH IN WRITING SHALL BIND LESSOR.

18. THE LESSEE STATES HE IS OVER 18 YEARS OF AGE.

CHAPTER 9

BORROWING MONEY, CREDIT USE AND MISUSE

Sources Of Loans

You may be able to borrow money from relatives, friends, business acquaintances, banks, credit unions, savings and loan associations. Advice — don't borrow from relatives; you have to live with them the rest of your life; friends, business acquaintances etc. you can always change; and when they hound you for money, you will change them.

Deadbeat

If you are going to be a producer, then you may become a deadbeat (naturally not from choice, merely from inability to pay debts). You may as well learn enough about being a deadbeat to survive the mental assaults of government tax collectors and private collection agencies.

Tough Collectors

Movie producers who have employees withhold a portion of the gross salary for U.S. income taxes, social security taxes, unemployment or disability taxes, etc. Sometimes the amount withheld is not paid to the appropriate government agency; instead the funds are used to complete the movie. Such action may subject the producer, their checkwriters, and some other involved persons to personal civil and/or criminal liability.

Sometimes producers don't pay actors or others appropriate union scale or other promised salary. This may cause the injured person and/or his union to harass the producer.

Exemptions, Etc.

A producer may (1) homestead his home, (2) lease instead of own his car, (3) keep the amount of money which his state laws exempt in a credit union and a federal savings and loan association, (4) study the other exemption statutes in his state and accordingly arrange his property, (5) try to avoid co-signing or guaranteeing loans and credit given to the film producing corporation, (6) promptly pay all tax and labor liabilities to avoid potential criminal charges.

Bank Loans

Sometimes a film is financed in part with money loaned by a bank to the producer. The bank probably won't be satisfied with merely the liability of the producing corporation (risky business), the producer (unstable), and the security of the film (if it does not earn enough to pay the bank loan on time, the film is not very good security).

Therefore the bank wants good credit risks to co-sign the loan: doctors, accountants, established businesses. The producer approaches these good credit risks with the promise, "If you co-sign the loan, you won't have to put up a cent when I make the picture and I will give you a profit participation in the picture." It is two years later, *if* the last has not been repaid, that these good co-signers have to "put up a cent" or more to repay the loan.

Financiers

Possibly, a financier may co-sign the bank loan. His terms may be: (1) Financier receives 3% interest on the principal of the loan, even though he did not lend the principal. (2) Financier is to be paid 2 years worth of interest in front out of the proceeds of the bank loan. (3) Financier determines in which studio the film is to be shot, which laboratory is to be used, and which lumber company will sell the lumber for the sets at what price, and your imagination can furnish alternative or additional side benefits such as which woman friend is to play what role.

Distributor May Co-Sign

The money lender may want the film distributor to co-sign or guarantee the loan. Depending on circumstances (the producer, the distributor, the film project) the distributor may sign. This signature may encourage the other co-signers to sign; these others may believe that the money lender will go after the distributor when the loan is due and the distributor will pay off the loan to avoid the money lender taking the film. Unfortunately for these other co-signers, the bank may simply take the easy way out and grab the accounts of any co-signers who are also depositors in the bank.

Avoid Fraud

The producer who persuades others to co-sign a bank loan providing proceeds to be used to make a picture, may be committing fraud in his statements to these co-signers. Do you remember key words of the elements of fraud: misrepresentation of material fact knowing that it was a misrepresentation and intending to deceive the victim, which victim was deceived, and acting on reliance on the misrepresentation suffered damages.

The producer must be careful to not make a misrepresentation: "This film will make money," or "you will never have to pay anthing to the bank," or "I will refinance the loan before the two years are up."

Many producers are in love with the glamor of films, with the concept that the picture they produce may be seen by over 50,000,000 Americans and over another 50,000,000 other Earthlings. Similarly, potential co-signers may be awed by the concept that the way 100,000,000 humans spend 90 minutes of their lives will depend on whether or not the co-signer gives his autograph on a bank note. Do you realize that 100,000,000 times 90 minutes equals more than 540 billion seconds?

Pessimism and Optimism

The producer may know that in the budget of the picture, which was approved by the money-lender and the distributor, there is no allocation for the payment of (1) advance interest payment to the financier, (2) later interest payment to the money lender, unfortunately for the producer, the (1) advance interest payment to the financier is frequently taken out of that portion of the budget which was called "Producer's Fee." Unfortunately for the co-signers, if the distributor does not pay (2) later interest payments to the money lenders, the money

49

lender may chase the co-signers.

The producer may wonder, "If I have to co-sign, pay interest if the distributor does not, pay the principal if the distributor does not, give up a portion of my producer's share to the financier to get enough money to have the picture shot, then why should I bother producing the picture in the first place?"

That's a good question.

One possible answer — Because you want to make films.

Second possible answer — Because you want to receive the cash left to you as the producer's fee.

Third answer — Because you may make a lot of money receiving your deferred income, your profit participation, your sale of various associated or subsidiary rights, your producing more pictures.

DON'T GIVE THE SAME SECURITY TWICE.

If you are not careful, you may find yourself promising the completed film copyrights and negative to (1) your private backers, (2) your money lenders, (3) your laboratory which extends credit, (4) your distributor.

Summary

Debts you incur to produce your film may include:

1. Debts to your backers if they have the choice to call their money either an investment or a loan.

2. Debt to money lenders.

3. Debt to the laboratory and equipment houses.

4. Deferrals for key people who accept part of their due in cash and part in the promise that the distributor will pay them eventually if the film earns enough.

5. Private debts incurred by the producer.

CHAPTER 10

PRIVACY AND LIBEL

Commandments

"Thou shalt not covet thy neighbor's house ... nor anything that is thy neighbor's."
"Thou shalt not bear false witness against thy neighbor."

Constitution

Sure, you have the constitutional right of free speech. And the people you wrong by appropriating their names, likeness etc. for commercial reasons, by invading their privacy, by slandering (oral defamation) or libelling (written defamation) can sue you. Sometimes truth is a defense, sometimes lack of malice is a defense, sometimes freedom of speech is a defense; but the law is so complicated that sometimes these are not defenses.

Confusion

You can't count on yesterday's decisions (precedents) in the fields of privacy and libel to give you an automatic victory in your lawsuit.

Before you exploit somebody's exciting story without obtaining adequate *releases* covering both truthful and fictitious versions of their stories, think — how would I like it if I were the victim?

Cartoons

The adult cartoon lessons which follow simplify and oversimplify parts of the laws of privacy and libel, and have a tremendous amount of information packed into them.

INVASION of
RIGHT OF PRIVACY
INCLUDES
①
INTRUSION UPON A PERSON'S PHYSICAL SOLITUDE

Peering into the windows of a home.

Persistent and unwanted telephone calls.

Unauthorized prying into plaintiff's bank account.

Eavesdropping on private conversations by wire tap.

INVASION of
RIGHT OF PRIVACY
INCLUDES
②

PUBLIC DISCLOSURE OF PRIVATE
FACTS ABOUT A PERSON'S LIFE.

A.
Defendant put a notice in his window
announcing to the world plaintiff
owed him money and would not pay.

B.
Motion picture revived the past
history and disclosed the present
identity of a reformed prostitute.

C.
Publicity was given to medical
pictures of plaintiff's intimate
anatomy.

D.
Publicity was given to a woman's
masculine characteristics and
eccentric behavior.

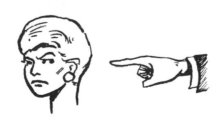

INVASION OF
RIGHT OF PRIVACY
INCLUDES
③

ACTS WHICH PLACE THE AFFECTED
PERSON IN A FALSE LIGHT IN THE
PUBLIC EYE.

A.
Lord Byron succeeded in
enjoining the circulation
of a bad poem which had
been attributed to his pen.

B.
Plaintiff's picture is
used to illustrate a book
or article with which he
has no reasonable
connection.
(Honest cab driver's face used in
article on "Cheating Cab Drivers.")

INVASION OF
RIGHT OF PRIVACY
INCLUDES
④

APPROPRIATION FOR COMMERCIAL BENEFIT OF A PERSON'S NAME, LIKENESS OR APPEARANCE.

A.

Defendant used a picture of a young and pulchitrudinous lady to advertise defendant's product without her consent.

B.

Insurance company used plaintiff's name and picture, as well as a spurious testimonial from him.

C.

Host who shot home movies that included guest who was a movie star showed these home movies on commercial television.

THAT'S ME!

RIGHT OF PUBLICITY

"yes! You may use my name, picture, plays and poses in your motion picture and to advertise the film...

"Yes, you may use my name, voice, likeness, picture on your sound recordings, labels and album covers, and to promote, publicize and advertise the records.

STAR JOHNNY MINUS

"yes... you may use my name, picture and testimonial about your product on radio, television, and publication advertising for a period of one year.

"yes, you may use the blurb: "I LIKE THIS BOOK... JOHNNY MINUS," ON THE U.S. Paperback edition of "RICK RICO RIDES.""

JOHNNY MINUS IN CRIME IN THE ALLEYS — NOW PLAYING

JOHNNY MINUS SINGS ONE MORE TIME! Stereo

Johnny Minus says "This Is The Tops"! RICK RICO RIDES by Ron Rich

COURTS DIFFER IN THEIR OPINIONS ON PUBLICITY...

THE RIGHT TO PUBLICITY IS A PERSONAL RIGHT BELONGING TO THE HUMAN BEING INVOLVED, AND WHEN HE DIES, THE RIGHT DIES.

THE RIGHT TO PUBLICITY IS A **PROPERTY** RIGHT, AND WHEN THE HUMAN BEING INVOLVED DIES, THE PROPERTY RIGHT BELONGS TO HIS HEIRS OR LEGATEES.

THE RIGHT OF PUBLICITY DEPENDS ON THE LAW OF EACH RESPECTIVE STATE.

THERE IS <u>NO</u> RIGHT TO PUBLICITY!

LIBEL

INCLUDES...
DAMAGE TO THE ESTEEM
OR SOCIAL STANDING IN WHICH
ONE IS HELD...

To print falsely that one has
been arrested for a crime.

To falsely claim that one is
heartless and neglectful of
his family...

LIBEL

INCLUDES...
DAMAGE THROUGH
RIDICULE...

TO SENSATIONALIZE THE POVERTY
OF A FORMER GENTLEWOMAN SO
AS TO BRING HER INTO CONTEMPT
AND RIDICULE...

TO MAKE A JOKE OUT OF THE
DESERTION OF A BRIDE ON
HER WEDDING DAY...

LIBEL
INCLUDES...
DAMAGE THROUGH WORDS
IMPUTING DISEASE OR MENTAL
ILLNESS...

To falsely attribute to an individual a disease which is loathsome, infectious or contagious...

"HE HAS THE PLAGUE!" "HE HAS LEPROSY!"
"HE HAS SMALL POX!"
"HE HAS A VENEREAL DISEASE!"

60

LIBEL

INCLUDES...
DAMAGING ONE IN HIS TRADE,
OCCUPATION OR
PROFESSION...

To falsely publish that a clergy-man was "an interloper, a meddler and a spreader of distrust."

To falsely publish that a school-teacher kept schoolgirls after school so he could court them.

To falsely publish that a jockey rode horses unfairly and dishonestly.

LIBEL

INCLUDES...

DAMAGE TO A CORPORATION'S
INTEGRITY, CREDIT, OR ABILITY
TO CARRY ON ITS BUSINESS...

To falsely state a company is in
shaky financial condition...

To falsely state a corporation
cannot pay its debts,

To falsely imply that a
corporation engages in
dishonest practices.

CHAPTER 11

UNIONS & UNION CONTRACTS

A contract between an employer and an employee involves the two parties.

A contract between an employer (the production company) and an employee (director, star, cameraman, etc.) may involve four parties: the employer, his trade association, the employee's union, the employee.

A production company may have an agreement with his trade association to abide by the provisions of the contracts between the trade association and various unions.

A union employee may have a contract with his union to abide by the provisions of the contract between the union and the employer's trade association. Actually, the employee promises to abide by the union constitution and by-laws.

There are very many unions in the motion picture and television industries.

Some unions have succeeded in persuading employers to pay wages and furnish fringe benefits which are quite expensive to these employers.

Some employers do not belong to employer groups which have signed contracts with unions.

These employers may hire non-union personnel or union personnel who hide the fact they are working for these employers from the employees' respective unions.

Each union has two basic purposes: (1) to preserve itself, (2) to help its members. Sometimes these two purposes are in conflict. Each employee of the union has three purposes: (1) to help himself, (2) to help the union, (3) to help the union members. Sometimes these three purposes conflict.

The employer group contracts with unions are frequently very long, very detailed, mention items such as minimum wages, fringe benefits, additional use payments, work hours, job descriptions, etc.

Unions which represent entertainers include Screen Actors Guild, Screen Extras Guild, American Guild of Variety Artists, American Federation of Musicians, American Federation of

Television and Recording Artists.

Other guilds include the Producers Guild, the Directors Guild, Writers Guild of America West, Inc., Dramatists Guild, etc.

Some of these guilds and unions have agreements with agents, which agents are then "franchised."

One of the worst mistakes a beginner can make is to join a union too early. By joining the union he promises to abide by union rules; if he violates the union rules by working for less than union scale the beginner can be fined by the union. If the beginner can't get a union job for a union employer (an employer who signed a contract with the union), and the beginner faces the possibility of a fine if he takes a job with a non-union employer, then the beginner is in trouble.

Similarly, a producer *may* find himself better off producing educational films, industrial films, and other films without signing with any and every union.

Some unions have a policy of insisting that all persons working on a film project are union members. This policy has caused a lot of producers to shoot films outside of the greater "Hollywood" area.

There are union jurisdictional fights which interfere with working opportunities of union members and interfere with production.

The pressures of unions (in union there is strength) and of union representatives have benefited union members while they are working.

Producers should try to read, know, and work within union contracts in order to avoid expensive hassles with the unions which may cause films to go over budgets.

CHAPTER 12

LABOR LAWS

There are federal labor laws and state labor laws.

Labor laws concern (1) employers—unions, (2) unions—employees, (3) employers—employees.

Employer v. Unions. Neither is supposed to commit any "unfair labor practice" against each other.

Unions v. Employees. Unions are supposed to help employees, not merely subjugate them. Employees are supposed to help unions, not steal from them or from pension funds.

Employers v. Employees. Employers are supposed to pay at least minimum wages; to pay over-time when appropriate, to keep records; to have special considerations for children; apprentices and women; to abide by health rules.

There is a theory that our combination of skilled labor and productive machines is able to produce all the consumer, agricultural, industrial and business items needed with only a fraction of the national work force. The rest of the available work force is therefore shuttled into (1) the legal inability to work such as children, (2) the reduced necessity for income through working full time such as senior citizens, (3) the pass-time jobs such as many civil and military government jobs, (4) the keep out of the labor market subsidies for students and people who don't want to work, (5) the spread-the-work jobs which management calls "featherbedding," (6) etc.

Under this policy, there are laws punishing employers who allow children to work; in some states these laws are applied against producers who allow child actors to work. In other states, child actors may work only with the approval of some governmental authority, and/or only a certain total number of hours a day during the school year, and/or with a school teacher providing a minimum hours of daily education.

Producers should keep extensive records of hours worked, and should pay employees fully in accordance with governmental and union regulations. When extensive records would show violations of governmental or union regulations, the employer may find himself in a mess.

Many producers avoid employing children because of these anti-child labor laws (both U.S. and state), because of the limited daily hours the children can work, because of the extra expenses for the school teacher and the child's adult companion, and because some children's mothers are pains who take up the producer's valuable time.

CHAPTER 13

WORKMEN'S COMPENSATION

Sometimes employees are hurt on the job. They may be hurt because of (1) their fault, (2) a fellow employee's fault, (3) the employer's fault, (4) an outsider's fault, (5) nobody's fault.

These employees can apply for Workmen's Compensation: (1) medical expenses, (2) allowance while they are not working, (3) if applicable permanent injury lump sum amount.

Employers are required, or strongly persuaded, or both, by law, directly or indirectly, to carry a Workmen's Compensation insurance policy. If the employer has no policy, he may find himself out of pocket for all the money awarded to the employee (and he *may* find criminal type charges brought against him in some states).

Sometimes persons hired as "independent contractors" may be hurt on the job, and may then claim that they were "employees" for Workmen's Compensation purposes. The employer, the insurance carrier, and the state boards hearing Workmen's Compensation hearings and appeals may agree with or disagree with this contention.

Employers frequently pay a premium to their insurance carrier at the beginning of the work year or work period. Afterwards the carrier may determine that the amount of payroll and type of work during the work year or work period entitled the insurance carrier to an amount which may be more or less than the premium paid at the beginning of the year.

Producers who are preparing a film budget should plan for the initial and later additional Workmen's Compensation premiums.

CHAPTER 14

INSURANCE

Producers can insure, or at least try to insure;
    (a) their own lives and health,
    (b) the lives and health of stars and other key persons,
    (c) that the picture will be completed on time (completion bond),
    (d) against rain and other weather conditions,
    (e) against property damage, fire, burglary, etc.
    (f) against damages and risks of other kinds,
    (g) Workmen's compensation.

Obtaining insurance can take a lot of time and can be very expensive.

Lots of producers decide to not take out all of these insurance coverages. This is risky.

The insurance companies prepare the insurance contracts. Frequently, insured persons are confused by the lengthy, small and difficult to read print. Insured persons may believe that they are covered for some contingency under Paragraph A, because they fail to understand the exclusion from coverage in paragraph K (4) (iii) part 2, subdivision 3.

CHAPTER 15

TAXES

Income Taxes

1. List total wages on Form 1040, page 1.
2. List dividend and interest income on Schedule B.
3. List total independent contractor income on Schedule C.
4. List house rental on Schedule E.
5. List various other income on various forms.
6. List various deductions on various forms ("personal" itemized deductions on Schedule A, business deductions on Schedule C., etc.)
7. Add here, subtract there, subtract some more for exemptions.
8. On a Form SE you can calculate any *social security taxes* you may have to pay on your Schedule C net income.
9. Eventually your calculations will bring you back to Form 1040, page 1, where you can calculate *U.S. income taxes.*

* * * * *

During the tax year you may have paid taxes by making quarterly payments directly to the Internal Revenue Service and/or by having taxes withheld from your wages.

Possibly you overpaid in advance; if so, you can request a refund of the overpayment.

Possibly you underpaid in advance; if so, you are supposed to pay the balance due to the Internal Revenue Service.

Does it sound complicated to you? Yes? You are right. It is complicated. But any person like you who can master concepts such as A + B roll printing, viewing systems of cameras, cinch marks on films, diffraction, super 8, single 8, regular 8, exposure, filters, workprints, release prints, plus diopters, ASA ratings of raw stock, tape recorders, parallax, zero printing, etc. can also understand (1) keeping checks, check stubs, bank statements, receipts, (2) making daily entries of all cost expenditures in a business daily diary, (3) keeping full details concerning entertaining for business purposes.

Tax Audits

During the first part of the year you prepare income tax returns. There are techniques to preparing tax returns.

Taxpayers sort receipts and checks. Taxpayers know that frequently taxpayers have tax-deductable expenses, but don't have any receipts and checks. For example: trade publications, entertainment, taxi and limousine rides to and from airports, payroll deductions for disability insurance and interest containing amounts paid to a credit union, work taxes, etc.

The tax return is prepared to accurately reflect expenses, whether or not receipts were kept.

The Internal Revenue Service computer in Ogden, Utah, and Internal Revenue Service humans are aware that entertainers are prime game for tax audits because many entertainers fail to keep checks, receipts, accurate daily records of business mileage and proof the mileage was for business reasons, etc.

The Internal Revenue Service makes money for itself when it disallows expenses and taxpayers have to pay more.

The Internal Revenue Service uses Office Audits and Field Audits. An Office Audit commences with an I.R.S. letter to the taxpayer in which the taxpayer is invited to bring receipts to a Tax Examiner in an I.R.S. office. In a Field Audit, the I.R.S. Revenue Agent visits the taxpayer.

The professional I.R.S. men frequently prefer to deal directly with taxpayers, who don't know tax law and can easily be bluffed by (1) truthful, (2) misleading though literaly truthful, (3) misleading statements of I.R.S. men.

Therefore some I.R.S. communications fail to mention that you, personally, need not meet them and that the audit can be handled for you by your representative.

In the event you are contacted by the I.R.S. by letter, by telephone, or in person, you may politely, and firmly, inform the I.R.S. that you want them to deal only with your representative. You have the constitutional right to be represented. Any encroachment on your constitutional rights by employees of the Internal Revenue Service may be due to the undue eagerness of the I.R.S. man (who may be reprimanded by his superior).

70

Only a few taxpayers are audited each year. Your time to prepare for an audit of your current year business expenses is during the current year.

The Internal Revenue Service auditor may want to see your bank statements. Each month as your bank returns your statement, identify each deposit (salary, fee, unemployment check, insurance recovery, gift from —, loan from —, repayment of loan from —, sale of equipment, etc.). The Internal Revenue Service is curious when a taxpayer reports $5,000 in taxable income and the bank deposits show $20,000 in deposits.

Please enter in your daily diary such items as: trade papers, coin telephone calls, parking, where you drove (miles + business reason), and other cash outlays.

Please keep proof of sale, payment, insurance of instruments, equipment, and anything else being depreciated on your tax return.

With this happy reminder we will end this letter — most tax returns are not audited — and an unhappy note — but can you count on the luck of never being audited?

ARE YOU LOOKING FOR A TAX LOSS?

We have heard an attractive sounding theory that some people look for a way to lose money, and that these people may be willing to invest money in a movie in order to lose that money. It is an interesting theory.

Some people in high tax brackets combine loves of glamor and gambling, with the ability of sharing their business losses with the taxing authorities. If a businessman who might pay $200,000 in taxes if he had not lost $100,000 in a movie venture, loses the $100,000 and thus lowers his taxes to $140,000, then the net loss to the businessman is computed as follows: Cash loss in glamorous gamble: $100,000. Tax savings: $60,000. NET real loss: $40,000.

There are tax laws called "tax ideas" by those who like them and "tax loopholes" by those who don't. (Investment credit. Cattle. Oil. Buildings.) Some of these may be useful to you. Others may lead you to be poor investments in which you lose your shirt to save tax dollars.

Property Taxes

You have heard about people being "land poor." They own land that they can't sell, but they have the burden of raising money to pay property taxes. Many entertainment industry persons who burdened themselves with big overhead and big properties suffer terribly because of the burden of property taxes. To avoid this burden, and other burdens of overhead, many producers rent, but don't own, shooting stages and locations, offices and equipment.

PRETEND YOU WORK FOR THE I.R.S.

You like your job. Your job is collecting money from creditors of Uncle Sam. A movie producer creditor withheld social security and federal income taxes from his employees, but failed to pay that withheld money to Uncle Sam. The creditor says he spent the money on completing a movie. The creditor begs you to not close down his business for failure to pay his taxes. You like your job. You like closing down businesses for failure to pay taxes.

Question — Would you close up the business? It may or may not help you collect money from this motion picture producer. You don't care whether it helps you collect money from this motion picture producer. If he pays up, fine, you have collected money. If he does not pay up, you close his business and scare another dozen motion picture producers into making their payments on time.

PRETEND YOU ARE A MOVIE PRODUCER

You have a limited budget for your picture. You employ above the line (director, actors, actresses) and below the line (cameramen, technical staff) personnel. You withhold (a) federal income tax, (b) federal social security, (c) state income tax, (d) state disability or unemployment insurance. You immediately deposit the amount withheld plus another 10% of gross salary (e) for employer's share of social security, (f) federal unemployment tax, (g) state unemployment insurance, (h) workmen's compensation into a TAX ACCOUNT in your bank.

You go over budget.

You try to get money from your investors, your bank, your friends, your relatives, You try to have your employees and creditors agree to wait for their money. You fail to get money. Your picture is unfinished.

You decide to steal. You decide to steal the withheld portion of your employees' salaries. You do steal the money out of the TAX ACCOUNT.

The time for you to pay the money in the TAX ACCOUNT to the federal and state government comes up. You don't have the money to pay. You don't pay.

The time for you to file a quarterly tax return concerning employees' wages, withheld wages, employers' taxes come up. Should you file the tax returns? If you do file the tax returns without at the same time paying your taxes, the government tax collectors will be alerted.

If you don't file the tax returns, then you will have to pay penalties for failure to file the tax returns.

PRETEND YOU WORK FOR A PRODUCER

You are a freelance photographer (still or motion picture) who uses his own equipment while working. OR, you are a freelance lightman who brings his own equipment. OR you are a freelance sound man who brings his own equipment. You are on the borderline between (a) an employee who is paid a salary (gross salary minus withheld taxes, withheld union dues, withheld Motion Picture Relief Fund contributions equal net salary, OR (b) an independent contractor who is paid a flat fee for his work. There are valid arguments placing you (a) as an employee or (b) as an independent contractor.

The movie producer gives you a choice. He will pay you $200 a day gross salary or $200 a day as a fee. This $200 is the total amount he will pay for your services and the use of your equipment.

Which do you want to be: (a) an employee OR (b) an independent contractor?

CHAPTER 16

"SELLING" MOVIES, MARKETS.

1. You, as the producer, may deal with a distributor (or you may be able to reserve certain rights and thus deal with several users).

2. The distributor will deal with:
- (a) sub-distributors
- (b) states righters
- (c) branches
- (d) exhibitor chains
- (e) individual exhibitors
- (f) non-theatrical film distribution companies
- (g) television distributors
- (h) other U.S. media distributors
- (i) foreign distributors
- (j) etc.

3. The sub-distributors, states-righters, branches and exhibitor chains must deal with exhibitors.

4. The exhibitors must deal with consumers. These dealings may concern:

(a) receipts for box office tickets.

(b) receipts for student's cards and for sales of cards and passes to other privileged characters.

(c) receipts from popcorn and other mouth area concessions.

(d) receipts from parking and other concessions.

The above are the bucks that are fought for between the exhibitors and the ones who furnish the films to the exhibitors.

The contract between an exhibitor and a distributor may provide, concerning receipts from sales of box office tickets:

(a) the distributor pays the exhibitor a lump sum for the use of his theatre (a so-called "four wall" deal), and the distributor keeps box office ticket sales receipts.

(b) the exhibitor pays the distributor a flat sum for the use of his film, and the exhibitor keeps box office ticket sales receipts.

(c) the exhibitor and distributor split box office ticket

sales in accordance with an agreed to percentage for each of them.

(d) the cost of advertising is deducted from box office ticket sales receipts; the rest is divided in accordance with an agreed to percentage.

(e) the cost of advertising and an agreed to amount for theatre overhead is deducted off the top; the excess, if any, is allocated mostly to the distributor and less so to the theatre.

(f) other methods and variations.

Sometimes there is cheating.

Some theatre patrons sneak into the theatre.

Some theatre personnel pocket box office receipts or set up a competetive system which routs customer's money into crooked pockets.

Some exhibitors lie about their receipts in order to reduce the amounts they report and pay to distributors. This lie is a breach of the exhibitor-distributor contract.

This lie is a misrepresentation. Sometimes exhibitors are sued for fraud by distributors. But, the sued exhibitors may decide to type out cross-complaints charging the distributors violated anti-trust laws. The best defense for strategy reasons is often a ruthless offense.

Distributors know their problems with each of their markets.

A distributor may refuse to distribute a film because he does not see how he can make a profit with the film.

A "peanut" budget "X" rated film may be useless to a distributor of "A" budget non "X" films.

An "A" budget picture may be horribly undersold by a distributor whose strength lies in selling low budget horror flicks to theatres for low fees.

The producer may find, much to his distress, that he has failed to provide in his distribution contract for the return of all rights, the negative and all prints, if the distributor fails to meet certain financial goals (i.e., fails to pay off the bank loan by one target date, the deferrals by another target date, minimum amounts to the producer on or before other dates).

The distributor won't bother distributing the film if the distributor can't make money by distributing the film.

Exhibitors don't want to play films, no matter how little the rental cost may be, if the films don't draw sufficient box office.

75

There are many films produced for commercial theatre release in mind which have had zero or only a few screenings in commercial theatres.

The producer may be able to receive initial investments in the film from potential markets — television, exhibitors, foreign exhibitors and television interests, etc.

The producer may receive such initial investments by (1) trading film profit particupation or ownership rights in the film, or by (2) collecting pre-paid amounts for film rental or territorial rights.

CHAPTER 17

DISTRIBUTION

Producer-Distributor Contract

If you were given $100,000, would you object? If you were given a $100,000 movie, would you object? If all you had to do to obtain distribution rights to $100,000 would be to offer some paperwork (namely, a producer-distributor contract) to the producer, would you do it?

Some distributors obtain all rights, for the territory of the world, for the period of twenty years, to movies which cost hundreds of thousands of dollars *without giving a single penny to the producer.*

Other distributors who are offered films on that basis reject the opportunity offered to them. Why? These distributors know that they will have to advance money for such items as (1) blowing up 16mm to 35mm, (2) advertising, press books, trailers, posters, (3) prints, and (4) overhead. The distributor divides his potential receipts into two sources: *first,* U.S. states righters and exhibitors, *second:* foreign, television, 16mm distributors, others. A distributor who does not anticipate receiving more money from his sources then he must spend in expenses, may reject the film even if it is offered to him without his having to pay a penny in front to the producer.

The distribution contract covers many items, including but not limited to the following:

1. The copyright in the movie, music, outtake, scripts, etc.

2. The physical exposed film, developed film, negatives, work prints, answer prints, prints for exhibition, sound tracks, tapes, etc.

3. The scope of distribution: commercial theatres (35mm), commercial theatres (16mm), schools, churches, institutions, collectors, etc. (16mm), cassettes and other video connected means, direct mail order sales to consumers, etc.

4. The territory: the world, U.S. & Canada, the 13 Western States.

5. The time period: 20 years, 10 years, forever, 3 years. This should provide for return of all prints and negatives at the end of that period.

6. The distributor's first bite herein irreverently called Bite One (30% of gross paid by theatres, 15% of gross paid by subdistributors and states righters, 25% from sales of all other rights and territories and means of distribution). These percentages are *not* given as ideal or correct; they are merely used to show that percentages can vary depending on what is being sold (or leased, licensed, rented, etc.). There should be a clause providing for 50% (or some other percentage) of all of distributor's receipts due to any commercial exploitation of the rights given to or enjoyed by distributor if the contract fails to mention how much of distributor's receipts for exploiting such right distributor is to pay to producer.

7. The distributor's second bite, (herein irreverently called Bite Two). This consists of taking out of the producer's share expenses which are paid by the distributor to do his job of distribution, such as costs for advertising, press books, trailers, prints, etc. Portions of this second bite are sometimes distributed in several places in the contract (rather than lumped together at one place so that the producer can see how big and perpetual — as the distributor keeps spending money for advertising and prints — the second bite is).

8. Royalty reports, royalties, auditing rights.

9. Other items.

If you were a distributor, and (1) if you had a producer willing to give you all his rights without receiving any cash advance, and (2) if this producer was willing to sign a contract pursuant to which you never had to pay him any royalties, would you (3) give the producer a cash advance and (4) give the producer any royalties?

Would you give a stranger a buck if you did not have to?

Distributor — Exhibitor Contract.

The distributor and the exhibitor have many items in their contract, including but not limited to:

1. Name of picture

2. Play dates of picture; exhibitor's options for additional weeks.

3. Play dates of trailer.

. 4. Manner of calculating the amount the exhibitor is supposed to pay the distributor. This amount could be a flat fee. Or the amount could be calculated. The calculations could be: (a) percentage(s) of box office receipts (candy counter receipts, parking fees, student ticket card fees, etc.), OR (b) percentage(s) of (various receipts less various expenses such as minimum theatre overhead and/or advertising expenses).

It is quite possible that box office returns as reported by the exhibitor may be less than the total of agreed theatre overhead and/or advertising expenses. Thus, the net amount payable by the exhibitor to the distributor may be $0.00.

The producer-distributor may provide that the cost of shipping prints is a Bite Two expense. If shipping prints cost $15.00, then the producer has lost $15.00 because the exhibitor reported to the distributor that the amount due to the distributor was $0.00.

Torts

So far in this chapter we mentioned law in its convenient classification of CONTRACTS. Now let us discuss the convenient classification of TORTS.

One of the TORTS is *fraud*. Another TORT is *negligence*.

If the distributor breaches the distributor-producer contract by rendering a fraudulent royalty statement, then the distributor can be sued for *breach of contract and for fraud*.

If the exhibitor breaches the exhibitor-distributor contract by rendering a false financial account of receipts and expenses, then the exhibitor can be sued for *breach of contract and for fraud*.

If the producer is negligent in shopping for distributors, or is negligent in his failure to try to negotiate for better terms or his failure to consult with an accountant who could foresee royalty traps or an attorney who can see other traps, then the producer might find himself sued by his backers with whom he entered into contracts for *breach of contract and negligence*.

Cheating

Distributor versus Exhibitor suits in which Distributors accuse Exhibitors of cheating in their reports of box office receipts are reported several times a year.

Exhibitors may not account for all the customers in the theatre because some people sneak in and (1) some employees short-circuit admission money into their own pockets and steal, (2) some exhibitors make honest errors and/or cheat.

Splitting The Pie

Let's follow a box office dollar paid by a customer for a double feature. If the theatre keeps 50c, the distributor receives 50c. If the distributor takes 20c as its Bite One and 20c as Bite Two, then the distributor pays out 10c. The producers of the double feature share the 10c, half (5c) for one producer, and half (5c) for the other producer.

If a producer receives 5c out of each box office $1; then the producer would receive $50,000 out of a box office of $1,000,000.

The above examples only illustrate the approach to estimating receipts; the examples don't use actual figures.

A distributor tries to persuade exhibitors to play the movie. Exhibitors want to play movies which attract many customers, and don't want to play movies which don't draw enough customers to bring a weekly net profit to the exhibitors.

If a producer's movie loses money for the first few exhibitors which play the movies, it is conceivable that the movie may never play in another theatre. The distributor may be able to recoup some of the money he advanced for advertising, prints, etc. with sales to television and other users. Out of such gross receipts, the distributor will take Bite One and Bite Two, leaving for the producer the sum of $0.00.

Costs Of Prints

If the distributor of a million dollar A picture orders 400 prints, then he can cover the 1000 most lucrative theatres in six months. If the distributor of a B Western or a horror picture orders 40 prints, or the distributor of an X cheap sexploitation picture orders 10 prints, then he can cover the country's 36 biggest markets in about 36 months. For each movie, the distributor tries to order neither too few nor too many prints.

However, the interests of the distributor and the producer may or may not coincide. The distributor may want to gross as much money as fast as possible, and to do so may order 200 prints for a movie which could have earned the same gross with only 100 prints. In either case, the distributor would receive the same amount as Bite One. But in the first case Bite Two has to include the cost of 200 prints (e.g., 200 prints x $700 = $140,000), while in the second case Bite Two has to include the cost of less than half that amount and the producer might have received the rest.

The producer who is offered a contract by a distributor should keep these facts and others in mind while negotiating changes in the proposed contract.

The amounts and figures given above are only provided to make illustrations more vivid, and they may not apply to your factual situation.

FORMS FOR STUDY NO. 1

PRODUCER-DISTRIBUTOR LICENSE AGREEMENT

THIS AGREEMENT, made this _____ day of _____, 19_____, by and between _____, having its principal offices at _____, hereinafter referred to as the LICENSOR AND/OR PRODUCER, and _____, having its principal office at _____, hereinafter referred to as the LICENSEE AND/OR DISTRIBUTOR.

WITNESSETH:

1. The LICENSOR hereby grants to the LICENSEE, and the LICENSEE accepts from the LICENSOR, upon the terms and conditions of this Agreement, the sole and exclusive License to distribute the following motion picture, hereinafter referred to as the PHOTOPLAY in commercial motion picture theatres only: _____. This license does NOT include, for example, TELEVISION and distribution in store front theatres.

2. TERRITORY: The territory covered by this Agreement herein granted shall consist of the following: U.S. (50 States and District of Columbia).

3. TERM: The term of this Agreement and the franchise herein granted shall be for a period of three (3) years from the date first above written.

4. ADVERTISING: Advertising accessories and trailers are available through _____. LICENSOR will furnish LICENSEE, gratis, f.o.b., its exchanges, its normal requirement

of pressbooks, or any other advertising material deemed necessary by LICENSOR. LICENSEE shall advance $1500.00 for these items, the money to be recouped off the top before computing LICENSEE's share of gross rentals.

5. CENSOR CUTS: The LICENSEE shall have the right to make any cuts in the PHOTOPLAY which may be required by any duly authorized censorship authority, at his cost. LICENSEE shall not exhibit the film where government authorities have expressly given warning that the film shall not be exhibited.

6. WARRANTIES AND INDEMNIFICATION: The LICENSOR warrants and represents that he has the full right, power and authority to make the grant contained in this Agreement, and that LICENSEE will quietly and peacefully enjoy and possess all of the rights and privileges herein granted to LICENSEE throughout the full term of this Agreement without claim, let, or hindrance on the part of any third party. LICENSOR expressly disclaims any warrant, concerning any action by any government, since governments are unpredictable.

7. ASSIGNMENT: LICENSEE agrees that it will not assign or transfer this Agreement without prior written consent of LICENSOR. Any attempted ASSIGNMENT shall terminate LICENSEE's rights but not duties.

8. PAYMENTS: LICENSOR agrees that the distribution fee to be charged by LICENSEE shall be (30%) thirty percent of all gross rentals obtained from exhibitor throughout the territory. LICENSEE reserves the right to use Sub-Distributors where needed, but such Sub-Distributor's share shall come out of LICENSEE's share. LICENSEE agrees to furnish LICENSOR with written detailed reports monthly and to pay any monies to LICENSOR pursuant to said reports.

9. PRINTS AND ADVANCES: (a) LICENSOR agrees to keep for himself one 35mm Answer Print of the PHOTOPLAY. LICENSEE further agrees to pay for the cost of additional 35mm positive prints of the PHOTOPLAY on the following terms:

(b) LICENSEE will furnish LICENSOR with each and every print which is withdrawn from commercial use because of wear and tear or any other reason immediately upon its being so withdrawn or 6 months after its latest commercial use, whichever is sooner.

(c) All NEGATIVES will continue to be owned by

LICENSOR and will be stored at the following Film Laboratories: _____. LICENSEE agrees to pay to said film laboratories $6,000 (Six Thousand Dollars) upon execution of this contract to help defray the cost of the blow-up from 16mm to 35mm. This money will be recouped off the top from the gross rentals before computing LICENSEE's share of gross rentals and before remittances are made to LICENSOR.

LICENSEE agrees to order 10 release prints as soon as a 35mm negative is available and to pay for all release prints, and to not order less than ten or more than fifteen (15) prints without the written consent of the LICENSOR. The payments to the laboratory advanced by LICENSEE will be recouped from the gross rentals before payments are made to LICENSOR. LICENSEE will send LICENSOR copies of all purchase orders, invoices, checks and correspondence concerning each and every print.

10. GENERAL CONDITIONS: Nothing contained in this Agreement shall be construed as constituting a joint venture or partnership between the parties hereto, and neither party shall have the authority to bind the other as its representative in any manner whatsoever unless otherwise expressly provided in this Agreement.

11. LICENSOR and his representatives may copy (and may use any photocopy type machine on LICENSEE's premises and will pay LICENSEE 10c per copy made on LICENSOR's machine) and inspect LICENSEE's files concerning PHOTOPLAY, including but not limited to all exhibition contracts, all print records, all preview, pressbook and other advertising records, all shipping and routing records concerning all prints, all correspondence in which the PHOTOPLAY is mentioned, bookkeeping records showing any income, any advance paid by LICENSEE (e.g. for advertising, blow-up, release prints). This copying and inspecting may be made during business hours as often as LICENSOR desires.

12. LICENSEE's rights under this contract shall terminate:

    (a) On one year from the date of this contract if LICENSOR has not received cash for himself from LICENSEE of at least $_____.

    (b) On two years from the date of this contract if LICENSOR has not received cash for himself from LICENSEE of at least $_____.

13. At the expiration of the contract, LICENSEE shall turn over to LICENSOR every negative, internegative, answer print, release, trailer, advertising material, of or concerning PHOTOPLAY. Since LICENSOR paid for all this material, even though LICENSEE has the obligation to initially advance funds therefore, the parties agree that all these items belong to LICENSOR.

14. Upon execution of this contract, LICENSEE shall pay LICENSOR an advance of ($) _____ thousand dollars.

IN WITNESS WHEREOF, the parties to this Agreement have set their hands, the day and year first above written.

_____   _____

PRODUCER/LICENSOR   DISTRIBUTOR/LICENSEE

CHAPTER 18

FEDERAL COMMUNICATIONS COMMISSION

Radio and television stations need licenses issued by the Federal Communications Commission. The airwaves belong to the public, and the privilege to use the airwaves by radio and television stations can be granted or denied by the F.C.C. The Federal Communications Commission and stations are governed by the Constitution (freedom of speech) by statutes passed by Congress (see Title 47, United States Codes), by F.C.C. regulations (see Title 47, Code of Federal Regulations), by F.C.C. decisions, reports, opinions, orders, actions.

On the following pages are reprints from Volume 23, Federal Communications Commission Reports. (For sale by the Superintendent of Documents, U.S. Government Printing Office, Washington, D.C. 20402. Price $5.50.) The Digests in Volume 23 were added for convenience, but are not part of the decisions or reports.

F.C.C. 70–457

BEFORE THE

FEDERAL COMMUNICATIONS COMMISSION

Washington, D.C. 20554

In the Matter of
Liability of Continental Broadcasting
Corp., Licensee of Radio Station WHOA,
Hato Rey, P.R.
For Forfeiture

Memorandum Opinion and Order

(Adopted April 29, 1970)

By the Commission: Commissioner Bartley absent.

1. The Commission has under consideration (1) its notice of apparent liability dated February 26, 1969, addressed to Continental Broadcasting Corp., licensee of radio station WHOA, Hato Rey, P.R., and (2) licensee's response to the notice of apparent liability dated March 26, 1969.

2. The notice of apparent liability in this proceeding was issued because of the licensee's apparent willful or repeated violations of the terms of the station license by repeatedly failing to keep records of the field intensity measurements at the monitoring points at least once each 7 days, section 73.113(a)(4)(b) by repeatedly failing to show in the operating log, at least once daily, the readings of the antenna base current meters, section 73.114(a)(3) by failing to show in the maintenance log, each day, the results of the daily observations of the tower lighting and the results of its quarterly check of the automatic tower lighting equipment as required by section 17.47(b), and section 73.114(b) by failing to show in the maintenance log the results of the required daily inspection of the transmitting equipment. The notice indicated that the licensee was subject to apparent forfeiture liability in the amount of $1,000 pursuant to section 503(b) of the Communications Act of 1934, as amended.

3. In response to the notice of apparent liability the licensee denies, in part, the violations as cited and requests that the forfeiture be rescinded or reduced. In support of its request, licensee states, in general, that it has experienced difficulty in obtaining qualified operators; that it is now in compliance with the rules; that it has taken corrective action to prevent recurrence of these violations in the future, and that a fine of $1,000 would be a hardship on the station. Although licensee admits violating the terms of the station license as well as sections 73.113(a)(4)(b) and 73.114(b) of the rules, it denies violating section 73.114(a)(3) of the rules as it was set forth in the notice of apparent liability.

23 F.C.C. 2d

4. As we have stated in the past, proof that the licensee has now taken corrective action and, thus, is in compliance with the Commission's rules, is not a proper basis to excuse violations of the rules. See *Executive Broadcasting Company*, 23 R.R. 893 (1962). Also, licensee's financial condition was fully considered when determining the amount set forth in the notice of apparent liability, and licensee has submitted nothing new as a basis for reduction of the forfeiture, insofar as that reason is concerned. However, licensee has submitted evidence that it did not violate section 73.114(a)(3) as charged in the notice. There, licensee was cited for two violations pursuant to section 73.114(a)(3), failure to record daily and quarterly observations of the tower lighting and lighting equipment. The failure to record in the operating log the result of the daily observation of the tower lighting is, in fact, a violation of section 73.113(a)(6) for which licensee was not charged. Accordingly, we will rescind the forfeiture on this portion of the charge; however, we will not relieve the licensee of liability for its failure to record the quarterly observations, for which it received proper notice. In relieving licensee of this liability, we wish to stress, however, that the licensee should have come forward with the information in its response to the original notice of violation. Licensee is reminded that it is responsible for compliance with all provisions of the Communications Act of 1934 and the Commission's rules promulgated thereunder, and that it will be expected to adopt procedures to prevent any future violations.

5. On the basis of the licensee's reply and all of the circumstances of the case, we have decided to reduce the forfeiture. Accordingly, *It is ordered,* That Continental Broadcasting Corp., licensee of radio station WHOA, Hato Rey, P.R., *Forfeit* to the United States the sum of $750 for repeated failure to observe the terms of the station license and sections 73.113(a)(4)(b), 73.114(b) and 73.114(a)(3) of the Commission's rules. Payment of the forfeiture may be made by mailing to the Commission a check or similar instrument drawn to the order of the Treasurer of the United States. Pursuant to section 504(b) of the Communications Act of 1934, as amended, and section 1.621 of Commission rules, an application for mitigation or remission of forfeiture may be filed within 30 days of the date of receipt of this memorandum opinion and order.

6. *It is further ordered,* That the Secretary of the Commission send a copy of this memorandum opinion and order by certified mail—return receipt requested to Continental Broadcasting Corp., licensee of radio station WHOA, Hato Rey, P.R.

FEDERAL COMMUNICATIONS COMMISSION,
BEN F. WAPLE, *Secretary.*

23 F.C.C. 2d

BEFORE THE

FEDERAL COMMUNICATIONS COMMISSION

WASHINGON, D.C.   20554

In Re Complaint by
THE COMMITTEE OF ONE MILLION
   Concerning Fairness Doctrine Re CBS

LEE EDWARDS, *Secretary,*
The Committee of One Million,
Washington, D.C.

DEAR MR. EDWARDS: Your letter to Chairman Burch dated February 6, 1970, concerning a recent CBS news special broadcast on November 18, 1969, has been forwarded to this office for reply.

In your letter you state that CBS refused to give your committee equal time to reply to the program which you allege presented an inaccurate picture of Communist China today and contained a statement by the announcer, Marvin Kalb, which you allege was, in substance, not true.

The selection and presentation of specific program material are responsibilities of the station licensee, and under the provisions of section 326 of the Communications Act the Commission is specifically prohibited from censoring broadcast material.

However, if a station presents one side of a controversial issue of public importance, it is required to afford reasonable opportunity for the presentation of contrasting views. This policy, known as the fairness doctrine, does not require that "equal time" be afforded for each side, as would be the case if a political candidate appeared on the air during his campaign. Instead, the broadcast licensee is required under the fairness doctrine to try to present contrasting views in its overall programing which, of course, includes statements or actions reported on news programs. Thus, both sides need not be given in a single broadcast or series of broadcasts, and no particular person or group is entitled to appear on the station, since it is the right of the public to be informed which the fairness doctrine is designed to assure rather than the right of any individual to broadcast his views. It is the responsibility of the broadcast licensee to determine whether a controversial issue of public importance has been presented and, if so, how best to present contrasting views on the issue. The Commission will review complaints to determine whether the licensee appears to have acted unreasonably or in bad faith. For your further information, we are enclosing a copy of the Commission's public notice of July 1, 1964, entitled "Applicability of the Fairness Doctrine in the Handling of Controversial Issues of Public Importance."

It would not appear on the basis of information presently before the Commission that CBS has failed on an overall basis to afford rea-

23 F.C.C. 2d

sonable opportunities for the presentation of conflicting views regarding the issues discussed in its program.

The Commission's policy with respect to possible review of program material by this agency is set forth in its letter of February 28, 1969, to the three major networks, a copy of which is enclosed. We stated therein:

> [T]he Commission has never examined news coverage as a censor might to determine whether it is fair in the sense of presenting the "truth" of an event as the Commission might see it. The question whether a news medium has been fair in covering a news event would turn on an evaluation of such matters as what occurred, what facts did the news medium have in its possession, what other facts should it reasonably have obtained, what did it actually report, etc.
>
> *   *   *   *   *   *   *
>
> But however appropriate such inquiries might be for critics or students of the mass media, they are not appropriate for this Government licensing agency. It is important that the public understand that the fairness doctrine is not concerned with fairness in this sense. This is not because such actual fairness is not important, but rather because its determination by a government agency is inconsistent with our concept of a free press. The Government would then be determining what is the "truth" in each news situation—what actually occurred and whether the licensee deviated too substantially from that "truth !" We do not sit as a review body of the "truth" concerning news events.

For your further information, enclosed are copies of the Commission's memorandum opinion and order regarding the "Hunger in America" program and the Commission's letter of November 20, 1969, concerning the Commission's policies with respect to news programs and commentaries.

It is hoped that the above will explain the Commission's policies in the general area of your complaint.

Sincerely yours,

WILLIAM B. RAY, *Chief,*
Complaints and Compliance Division
for Chief, Broadcast Bureau.

23 F.C.C. 2d

EX PARTE COMMUNICATIONS BY STRANGERS

ADDITION OF A DISQUALIFYING ISSUE AS TO VIOLATIONS OF SEC. 1.1221 AND 1.1225 DE-NIED SINCE THE EX PARTE PRESENTATIONS WERE UNINTENDED AND DUE TO A MISUN-DERSTANDING, AND THE CANDOR AND COOPERATION OF COUNSEL FOR THE PARTY CHARGED MITIGATES THE GRAVITY OF THE VIOLATION. *AMER. B/CING COS.* 136

ALLEGED EX PARTE COMMUNICATIONS BY A LICENSEE IN VIOLATION OF SEC. 1.1221 AND 1.1225 ARE BEING CONSIDERED IN ANOTHER PROCEEDING (DOCKET 18606) AND, THEREFORE, ARE NOT CONSIDERED HERE. *WESTERN T/CERS, INC.* 242

FACILITY MAJOR CHANGE OF

APPLICATION FOR CHANGE (SEC. 1.572(A)) IN ANTENNA SITE AND HEIGHT DESIGNATED FOR HEARING ON AREAS OF GAIN AND LOSS AND UHF IMPACT SINCE THE PROPOSED OPERATION WOULD PLACE A PREDICTED GRADE B SIGNAL OVER THREE ENTIRE CITIES FOR THE FIRST TIME. *JEFFERSON STANDARD B/CING CO.* 931

FACTUAL ISSUES, DESIGNATED

PETITIONS FOR RECONSIDERATION OF AN ORDER REQUIRING THAT FACTUAL DETER-MINATIONS BE MADE BEFORE ISSUES OF LAW ARE DECIDED IN THE POLE LINE AT-TACHMENT PROCEEDING (22 FCC 2D 10) DENIED, SINCE MORE INFORMATION IS NEEDED TO MAKE A LEGAL DECISION. *CALIF. WATER & TEL. CO.* 840

FAIRNESS DOCTRINE

NEWS COVERAGE WILL NOT BE EXAMINED TO DETERMINE WHETHER IT IS FAIR IN THE SENSE OF PRESENTING THE TRUTH, SINCE THIS WOULD BE INCONSISTENT WITH THE CON-CEPT OF A FREE PRESS. *FAIRNESS DOCTRINE* 48

FAIRNESS DOCTRINE APPROPRIATE SPOKESMAN

EDITORIALS ON A SCHOOL LEVY ISSUE TO BE VOTED ON HELD TO BE A CONTROVER-SIAL ISSUE OF PUBLIC IMPORTANCE, AND THE STATIONS OBLIGATION WAS NOT MET MERELY BY CITING THE EXISTENCE OF DIFFERING GROUPS. THE FACT THAT THOSE WITH DIFFERING VIEWS ARE MEMBERS OF CONFIDENTIAL GROUPS DOES NOT RELIEVE THE STATION OF ITS OBLIGATION. *FAIRNESS DOCTRINE* 41

THE FAIRNESS DOCTRINE APPLIES TO THE SITUATION WHERE A SPOKESMAN FOR CAN-DIDATE A BUYS STATION TIME AND THE CAMPAIGN ISSUES AND/OR THE CANDIDATE ARE DISCUSSED, AND A SPOKESMAN FOR CANDIDATE B REQUESTS TIME UNDER THE FAIR-NESS DOCTRINE. HOWEVER, THE STATION IS NOT OBLIGATED TO FURNISH FREE TIME TO THE SPOKESMAN OF CANDIDATE B. *FAIRNESS DOCTRINE RULING* 707

THE FAIRNESS DOCTRINE APPLIES TO THE SITUATION WHERE A STATION SELLS TIME TO A SUPPORTER OF CANDIDATE A AND THE TIME IS USED TO CRITICIZE CANDIDATE B OR HIS POSITION ON THE ISSUES, AND A SUPPORTER OF CANDIDATE B REQUESTS TIME UNDER THE FAIRNESS DOCTRINE. THE STATION IS NOT REQUIRED TO FURNISH FREE TIME TO THE SUPPORTERS OF CANDIDATE B. *FAIRNESS DOCTRINE RULING* 707

FAIRNESS DOCTRINE CONTRASTING VIEWPOINT DUTY TO ENCOURAGE

SERIES OF THREE PROGRAMS ON A PROPOSED TOWN CHARTER ISSUE HELD TO BE A CONTROVERSIAL ISSUE OF PUBLIC IMPORTANCE REQUIRING PRESENTATION OF CON-TRASTING VIEWPOINTS, AND AN INVITATION TO APPEAR ONE DAY BEFORE AN ELECTION, WHERE PREVIOUS REQUESTS FOR TIME HAD BEEN DENIED, DID NOT CONSTITUTE COM-PLIANCE WITH THE FAIRNESS DOCTRINE. *FAIRNESS DOCTRINE* 45

IF NO APPROPRIATE SPOKESMEN COME FORWARD TO REPLY TO A CONTROVERSIAL ISSUE BY USE OF THE ANNOUNCEMENT TECHNIQUE THEREAFTER THE LICENSEE MUST CONTACT SPECIFIC PERSONS WHO APPEAR TO BE APPROPRIATE SPOKESMEN AND OFFER THEM A CLEAR AND UNAMBIGUOUS OPPORTUNITY TO RESPOND. *FAIRNESS DOCTRINE* 27

FAIRNESS DOCTRINE CONTRASTING VIEWPOINT EXPRESSION OF

LICENSEE HELD TO BE IN COMPLIANCE WITH THE FAIRNESS DOCTRINE IN OVERALL PROGRAMMING RE PRESENTATION OF CONTRASTING VIEWPOINTS ON THE ISSUE OF BIRTH CONTROL. UNDER SEC. 326, SELECTION OF SPECIFIC PROGRAM MATERIAL IS THE RESPONSIBILITY OF THE LICENSEE SINCE THE COMMISSION IS PROHIBITED FROM CENSORING THE MATERIAL BROADCAST. *FAIRNESS DOCTRINE* 50

WHERE A STATION WHICH HAD PREVIOUSLY PRESENTED THE AMBASSADOR OF ISRAEL AS A GUEST, PRESENTED CONTRASTING VIEWS IN ITS OVERALL PROGRAMMING AND HAS STATED AN INTENTION TO INVITE AN ARAB AMBASSADOR TO APPEAR ON AN INTERVIEW SHOW IF ONE SHOULD VISIT THE CITY, THERE HAS BEEN NO VIOLATION OF THE FAIRNESS DOCTRINE. *FAIRNESS DOCTRINE RULING* 705

FAIRNESS DOCTRINE CONTROVERSIAL ISSUE

LICENSEE FOUND TO HAVE COMPLIED WITH THE FAIRNESS DOCTRINE IN TERMS OF OVERALL PERFORMANCE, SINCE REASONABLENESS IN PRESENTING OPPOSING VIEWPOINTS DOES NOT REQUIRE ABSOLUTE EQUALITY IN ALLOCATION OF TIME. ALLEGATION OF DELIBERATE DISTORTION OF NEWS MUST BE ACCOMPANIED BY SIGNIFICANT EXTRINSIC EVIDENCE. *FAIRNESS DOCTRINE* 35

LICENSEE HELD TO BE IN COMPLIANCE WITH THE FAIRNESS DOCTRINE IN OVERALL PROGRAMMING RE PRESENTATION OF CONTRASTING VIEWPOINTS ON THE ISSUE OF BIRTH CONTROL. UNDER SEC. 326, SELECTION OF SPECIFIC PROGRAM MATERIAL IS THE RESPONSIBILITY OF THE LICENSEE SINCE THE COMMISSION IS PROHIBITED FROM CENSORING THE MATERIAL BROADCAST. *FAIRNESS DOCTRINE* 50

THE PROGRAM, HUNGER, A NATIONAL DISGRACE, HELD NOT TO BE A CONTROVERSIAL ISSUE OF PUBLIC IMPORTANCE, SINCE THE EMPHASIS OF THE PROGRAM WAS HOW TO END HUNGER AND NOT WHETHER HUNGER IS A NATIONAL DISGRACE. *FAIRNESS DOCTRINE* 33

EDITORIALS ON A SCHOOL LEVY ISSUE TO BE VOTED ON HELD TO BE A CONTROVERSIAL ISSUE OF PUBLIC IMPORTANCE, AND THE STATIONS OBLIGATION WAS NOT MET MERELY BY CITING THE EXISTENCE OF DIFFERING GROUPS. THE FACT THAT THOSE WITH DIFFERING VIEWS ARE MEMBERS OF CONFIDENTIAL GROUPS DOES NOT RELIEVE THE STATION OF ITS OBLIGATION. *FAIRNESS DOCTRINE* 41

MERE PRESENTATION OF AN EDITORIAL DISCUSSING THE NEED FOR CERTAIN INNOCULATIONS DOES NOT IN AND OF ITSELF ESTABLISH THE PRESENTATION OF A CONTROVERSIAL ISSUE OR PUBLIC IMPORTANCE. ASSERTIONS OF A CONTROVERSIAL ISSUE MUST BE SUBSTANTIATED. *FAIRNESS DOCTRINE* 60

SERIES OF THREE PROGRAMS ON A PROPOSED TOWN CHARTER ISSUE HELD TO BE A CONTROVERSIAL ISSUE OF PUBLIC IMPORTANCE REQUIRING PRESENTATION OF CONTRASTING VIEWPOINTS, AND AN INVITATION TO APPEAR ONE DAY BEFORE AN ELECTION, WHERE PREVIOUS REQUESTS FOR TIME HAD BEEN DENIED, DID NOT CONSTITUTE COMPLIANCE WITH THE FAIRNESS DOCTRINE. *FAIRNESS DOCTRINE* 45

LICENSEE DID NOT ACT UNREASONABLY IN REFUSING COMPLAINANT TIME TO RESPOND TO AN EDITORIAL SINCE THE VIEWS EXPRESSED WERE NOT OF A CONTROVERSIAL NATURE IN THAT THEY URGED LAWFUL CONDUCT RATHER THAN DISCUSSING THE MERITS OF THE SUPREME COURT DESEGREGATION ORDER. *FAIRNESS DOCTRINE RULING* 289

WHETHER THE CONSTITUTIONALITY OF THE REVISION COMMITTEE FOR THE VIRGINIA CONSTITUTION WAS A CONTROVERSIAL ISSUE IS A MATTER LEFT TO THE LICENSEES DISCRETION. ABSENT EVIDENCE THAT LICENSEE ACTED EITHER UNREASONABLY OR IN BAD FAITH, THE LICENSEES PROGRAMMING JUDGEMENT WILL BE UPHELD. *FAIRNESS DOCTRINE RULING* 876

FAIRNESS DOCTRINE EDITORIALIZING BY LICENSEE

MERE PRESENTATION OF AN EDITORIAL DISCUSSING THE NEED FOR CERTAIN INNOCULATIONS DOES NOT IN AND OF ITSELF ESTABLISH THE PRESENTATION OF A CONTROVERSIAL ISSUE OR PUBLIC IMPORTANCE. ASSERTIONS OF A CONTROVERSIAL ISSUE MUST BE SUBSTANTIATED. *FAIRNESS DOCTRINE* 60

91

CHAPTER 19

THE SEAMLESS WEB

One act ties into another. Law and business knowledge intertwine. The same act may subject the actor (the one who acts) to liability, civil and criminal liability.

We have discussed some topics a little bit — contracts, torts, copyright, obscenity, partnerships, corporations, creditors rights, debtors rights, privacy, libel, unions, labor law, Workmen's Compensation, insurance, taxes, Federal Communications Commission, etc.

You now know more than you did before. You have enjoyed, we hope, an introduction to film and television law. You have, we hope, an awareness which will allow you to avoid some legal problems.

We suggest you visit your county's law library, which probably is in or near the county courthouse, and which is or should be open to the public.

Ask to see the books mentioned in the bibliography in this volume.

CHAPTER 20

COPYRIGHT QUESTIONS AND ANSWERS

Copyright Questions And Answers

QUESTION 1
Why should I study law?

ANSWER
You, as a film student are governed by the law, and you will be continued to be governed by the law the rest of your life both in your film industry activities and in your other activities.

A little knowledge of the law may (a) help you comply with laws, (b) help you avoid trouble caused by your failure to comply with laws, (c) help you understand when to go to a lawyer who may know more, (d) *help you understand what the lawyer is talking about and how to comply with his advice.*

QUESTION 2
What are some of the areas of law?

ANSWER
Law has been called a "seamless web." Law schools have, for convenience of teaching students, different courses on (a) criminal law, (b) contract law, (c) tort law, (d) real property law, (e) copyright law, (f) partnership law, (g) corporation law, and (h) other courses.

Law book publishers have published individual books on such subjects as (a) libel, (b) first amendment rights, (c) motion picture contracts, (d) family law, (e) the right of privacy, (f) agency law, (g) labor law, and (h) other subjects.

QUESTION 3
Am I going to have to learn all about all those subjects?
ANSWER
No.

Frankly, there is probably nobody who knows *all* about

any of those subjects.

You will learn a little about a few of these areas.

If you have learned the knowledge available in this book, you will know a lot that most non-show business attorneys know.

QUESTION 4

Why is the word *"copyright"* followed by a *year* followed by the *name of some person or company* in movie credits, in books, in magazines, on maps, and elsewhere?

ANSWER

You have mentioned the three components of statutory *copyright notice*. Please, please remember the words *copyright notice* and the three elements:

FIRST ELEMENT:

The word copyright or the abbreviation copy or c in a circle ©

SECOND ELEMENT:

The year. Usually the year is shown in "Arabic" figures: 1974. Movies sometimes show the year with "Roman" figures: MCMLXXIV

THIRD ELEMENT:

The name of the copyright proprietor. A book's copyright is sometimes taken out in the name of the author, and is sometimes taken out in the name of the publisher. A movie's copyright is sometimes taken out in the name of the producing corporation or in the name of the distribution corporation.

The United States Copyright Act provides that the placing of the appropriate copyright notice is necessary to protect a "published" work with the protection of the U.S. Copyright Act.

If a work is "published" without proper *copyright notice* then the work is not protected by the U.S. Copyright Act.

QUESTION 5

What does "published" mean?

ANSWER

"Published" has different meanings for different purposes. In the case of books in the Copyright Act sense, it means "made available to the public" such as through sales by mail or in retail

94

stores to anyone who wants to buy the book.

Please look at the page on the reverse side of the title page of this book for the *copyright notice*. Does it say "© Copyright 1972 by Walter E. Hurst. All Rights Reserved. Manufactured In the United States of America" or similar words?

Remember the necessary sequence of events:

FIRST: The *copyright notice* is part of the copy given to the printer on the title page or the reverse side of the title page.

SECOND: The book is printed.

THIRD: The book is made available to the public ("published").

FOURTH: The book is registered with the Copyright Office.

QUESTION 6

What do I do to register a book with the Copyright Office?

ANSWER

Please see Form A from the Copyright Office which is used to register books.

WARNING

By the time you read this book, any of the forms mentioned in this book may be out of date. For current free circulars and free forms, you can write to: Register of Copyrights, Library of Congress, Washington, D.C. 20540.

QUESTION 7

I have not written a book, only a movie script. Can I register my script with the Copyright Office?

ANSWER

You are going to receive another "let's do research" type answer. See Form C.

QUESTION 8

I have written several good songs for my movie. I plan to play them to potential backers of my movie. Can I register the songs with the Copyright Office now?

ANSWER

Yes. See Form E.

QUESTION 9

When I have completed my movie, (a) *can* I register it with the Copyright Office? (b) *must* I register it with the Copyright Office.

ANSWER

Again we pass the answer back to that government agency about which activities you are asking, the Copyright Office. Ask for Form L-M and the letter-agreement concerning deposit of movies.

QUESTION 10

In addition to registering books, scripts, songs, movies, what else does the Copyright Office register?

ANSWER

The following list of Forms provides the major categories.

A.	Books
B.	Periodicals
C.	Oral Delivery Works
D.	Dramatic Works
E.	Musical Compositions
F.	Maps
G.	Works of Art
H.	Reproductions of Works of Art
J.	Photographs
K.	Prints
L — M.	Motion Pictures
N.	Sound Recording.

There are other classes.

QUESTION 11

What else does the Copyright Office do?

ANSWER

The Copyright Office publishes catalogs listing registrations. The catalogs cover semi-annual periods (January-June, July-December). Additional cumulative catalogs cover registrations over longer periods of time. Current and some older Copyright Office catalogs are available for low dollar amounts. Look for the motion picture catalogs in libraries of larger movie companies, law libraries, county public libraries.

You may wish to buy your own set for various reasons (for example, so that you can search to see whether anyone has registered a movie with a title identical to or very similar to the title you wnat to use for your movie). (Sometimes a search is made to see whether a movie is in the *public domain*.)

Each two years, the Copyright Office publishes an inexpensive law book which contains recent copyright cases. Some of these cases concern big names or well known works, and make interesting reading in addition to providing copyright law information. Be sure that your lawyer has a set of these Copyright Office law books in his office or otherwise available to him.

The Copyright Office, for an hourly fee, will search its records to ascertain what registrations have been made. For example, you may want to learn whether a prospective title you want to use has been used before not only (a) for another movie, but also (b) for a book, magazine, magazine story, song, or other class of work registered in the Copyright Office.

Concerning other activities, you can ask the Copyright Office.

QUESTION 12   QUESTION 12

Since you are writing the questions in this book, why don't you also write the complete answer? Why do you keep telling us to go elsewhere for more information?

ANSWER

This book is intended to introduce you to law. There is so much law that I can't possibly give you all of it. All I can do is give you introductory, usable information, which you need now, and leads to further information which you may need in the future.

For example, when you run into a copyright question in the future, you can start your search for knowledge in this book.

If you have followed past suggestions by getting (or knowing where you can read) the information sources mentioned in this book, then you can go to these sources of information.

For copyright information, you can also read (among others):

1. Nimmer On Copyright.

2. Corpus Juris Secundum.

3. American Jurisprudence 2d.

4. Title 17, United States Code (Copyright).

5. Copyright Office Regulations.

6. Rules Adopted By The Supreme Court — For Practice and Procedure Under Section 25 of an Act . . . Respecting Copyright.

7. Bulletin Of the Copyright Society.

8. ASCAP Copyright Law Symposium.

9. (The list is not ever complete).

QUESTION 13

I have not registered with the Copyright Office my (a) original story and my synopsis, (b) screen treatment, (c) script, (d) any of my letters to friends and relatives, (e) my office memorandum to my employees, (f) the song I am writing, (g) the paintings in my private workshop. Are these works protected by copyright even though I have not registered them with the Copyright Office?

ANSWER

Remember in the earlier answers when words like *copyright notice* and *published* were italicized? The question of timing is important.

Initially, before a work is *published*, it is protected by "common law" copyright. Once the work is *published*, it loses "common law" copyright.

If when the work is *published* it contains appropriate *copyright notice*, then the work is protected by "statutory" copyright.

Initially: pre-publication — "common law" copyright

Then: post-publication — "statutory" copyright.

"Common law" copyright protection is given to unpublished literary, artistic, and musical work, including such as the types of work as are listed in your question: (a) original story synopsis, (b) screen treatment, (c) script, (d) letters, (e) office memorandum, (f) songs, (g) paintings.

"Common law" copyright is that judge made law (in a few states there may be statutes about copyright protection *before* publication) which governs the right to prevent copying unpublished literary, artistic, and musical material.

Section 2 of the U.S. Copyright Act states: RIGHTS OF

AUTHOR OR PROPRIETOR OF UNPUBLISHED WORK. — Nothing in this title shall be construed to annul or limit the right of the author or proprietor of an unpublished work, at common law or in equity, to prevent the copying, publication, or use of such unpublished work without his consent, and to obtain damages therefor.

QUESTION 14

Is "common law" copyright *identical* in every state?

ANSWER

No.

QUESTION 15

Is "common law" copyright *different* in every state?

ANSWER

No.

QUESTION 16

Are you trying to confuse me about laws being neither *identical* nor *different* in every state?

ANSWER

No. You are just being introduced to another aspect of law in this United States and in these 50 states.

"Common law" copyright is generally judge made law. A judge has to decide which of two or more litigants in front of him is right. The judge researches the law as set forth in legislation and in previous court decisions. Then the judge selects that law which he feels applies to the facts in front of him, and the judge renders his decision.

You have heard of cases in which the U.S. Supreme Court rendered a decision in which not all Supreme Court justices agreed. The Supreme Court may have been split 5—4 or 6—3 or in other ways. These learned judges disagreed because the majority and minority emphasized different facts and/or different law.

Similar to Supreme Court justices being unable to agreee on the law is the situation of judges in different courts. Even though a judge hearing one case in Illinois and a judge hearing another case in California may have different litigants, the two cases may have a common legal issue (is common law copyright in a song lost if song is recorded on phonograph records and the records are made available to the public?)

Even after courts in one or more states have ruled on the issue, when it comes up in court in yet another state that court *may* say "YES" and court in yet another state *may* say "NO."

There are federal courts (Supreme Court, Courts of Appeal for different circuits, District Courts in different states and geographic areas in some states), state courts (trial courts and courts of appeal in each state), and additional courts to those mentioned in the parentheses.

SUMMARY

(a) *Common law copyright law* may differ in different states and federal circuits.

(b) On most *common law copyright law questions*, the law is the same or nearly so in most or all states and federal circuits.

(c) The *U.S. Copyright Act* applies to *published* works and to unpublished works *registered* with the Copyright Office.

(d) On most *U.S. Copyright Act questions*, the law is the same or nearly so in most or all federal districts and circuits.

QUESTION 17

Is Mark Twain's book "Tom Sawyer" still protected by copyright?

ANSWER

No. The book was published. The period of copyright protection has expired.

QUESTION 18

If an old original manuscript written by Mark Twain is discovered, is that manuscript still protected by copyright?

ANSWER

Yes. The manuscript is still covered by common law copyright.

QUESTION 19

Is the motion picture "Tom Sawyer" which was produced in the 1930s still protected by copyright?

ANSWER

Probably "yes." You can look into the question by

100

checking Copyright Office registrations. See whether the copyright claim in the motion picture was registered with the Copyright Office. Then see whether a Form R (R for Renewal) was duly filed in the Copyright Office approximately 28 years later.

QUESTION 20
How long is a copyright good for? What is the duration of a copyright?

ANSWER
Let's first discuss "common law" copyright. Then let's discuss 'statutory" copyright.

"Common law" copyright commences when the work (letter, manuscript, play, song, etc.) is created. It terminates if one of the following occurs. As long as none of the following occur, "common law" copyright continues. The following terminations of "common law" copyright are:

1. Publication
2. Dedication to the public
3. When the owner takes out statutory copyright (registers or deposits an unpublished work with the Copyright Office)

"Statutory" copyright, under the U.S. Copyright Act, commences with (a) *publication* with appropriate *copyright notice*, (b) *registration* of a claim to copyright with the Copyright Office.

"Statutory" copyright is good for an *initial term of* 28 years.

"Statutory" copyright has provisions about a *renewal term* of 28 years.

Since 1962, Congress has passed a series of laws continuing certain renewal terms for additional years.

The Copyright Office has issued Form R.

QUESTION 21
What are key items I should know about copyright protection in foreign countries.

ANSWER
Key Item 1. In your copyright notices (e.g., Copyright 1974 by William Storm Hale) always use the c in the circle (© 1974 by William Storm Hale). Protection in the United States

101

can be obtained by using either "Copyright" or "©" or both. Protection in over 50 countries belonging to the Universal Copyright Convention can be obtained if the "©" is used. Possibly the best practice is to use both © and Copyright. (e.g., Copyright © 1974 by William Storm Hale.)

Key Item 2. A lot of material (songs, books, etc.) from foreign sources may be in the public domain (not protected by copyright) in the United States, but may still be protected in another country under its copyright laws. If you use such foreign material as the basis of a movie you make, you may find that you can't release the movie in a country which still protects the underlying material without first making peace with the foreign copyright owner.

Key Item 3. There are many confusing judicial decisions concerning the extent of protection of foreign works in the United States. You may be able to copy a composition legally, but may not be allowed to copy a specific recording of a composition.

Key Item 4. Very few lawyers know copyright. Very few copyright lawyers know foreign copyright. Your copyright lawyer is going to have to spend a lot of time researching copyright when you ask him to investigate the legal aspects of your possibly pirating foreign literary, artistic and musical works.

Key Item 5. Foreign works which are not protected by copyright are a valuable source of material for movie makers. Many American book publishers and movie makers have made fortunes using foreign source materials not protected by copyright in the United States.

QUESTION 22

What are some of the reading materials concerning international and foreign copyright protection?

ANSWER

(a) Section 9 of Title 17, United States Code, Copyright, which lists treaties, sets forth the Universal Copyright Convention, etc.

(b) BULLETIN OF THE COPYRIGHT SOCIETY OF THE USA, New York University Law Center, 40 Washington Square South, New York, N.Y. 10011.

(c) COPYRIGHT BULLETIN, UNESCO Publications

Center, P.O. Box 433, New York, N.Y. 10016.

(d) COPYRIGHT. World Intellectual Property Organization (WIPO), 32, chemin des Colombettes (Placede Nations) 1211 Geneva 20 (Switzerland).

(e) Copyright Office Circular 38A, International Copyright Relations of the United States.

QUESTION 23

If I write a script for myself, do I own the common law copyright on the script?

ANSWER

Yes.

QUESTION 24

Should I register my screen play script with the Copyright Office?

ANSWER

That is up to you. Registration takes time and money. The registration fee now (1972) is $6.00. By registering the script with the Copyright Office, you may be able to prove that at least as of a certain date that screenplay script was written. Sometimes proving that a script was written on or before a specific date is important in lawsuits against somebody you claim infringed on (copied, printed) your script.

QUESTION 25

Should I send a copy of my script to myself by registered mail?

ANSWER

If you want to do so. Lots of people do that and feel fine about it. The question is: What are you going to do with the unopened envelope containing your script? Are you going to open that envelope (a) in front of *your* lawyer so that he believes you, (b) or in front of your lawyer and the *opposition* lawyer at a deposition so that the opposition lawyer and his clients believe you, (c) or are you going to keep the envelope unopened until you are in *court*?

If you do follow the script-in-registered-envelope path, attach the returned envelope to an identical copy of the script which is in the envelope. Otherwise, how are you going to be able to tell what script is in the envelope?

By the way, if you register a script with the Copyright Office, the Copyright Office will return to you pages 3-4 of Form C. Be sure to attach a copy of the script you registered to said returned pages 3-4 (or a photocopy of pages 3-4 in the event you keep pages 3-4 in your safe deposit box).

Some persons register their scripts with the WRITERS GUILD OF AMERICA WEST, INC., 8955 Beverly Boulevard, Los Angeles, California.

Most people don't bother to register their scripts with anyone.

There is no single system (registered mail, Copyright Office, Writers Guild, no registration) which is *the* best system for everybody and every script.

QUESTION 26

After I wrote a first draft of a script, I showed it to a friend who made suggestions on how to improve the script. Is my friend entitled to any compensation? Is my friend now a co-writer with me?

ANSWER

Let's ask more questions: What do you think? What does your friend think? Have you and your friends discussed the matter *orally*? Have you and your friend agreed on anything *orally*? Have you and your friend agreed to anything in *writing*?

You might achieve two purposes at once by having anyone who reads your script sign "a piece of paper." Purpose No. 1 — to establish that as of a certain date the script had been written. Purpose No. 2 — to have your friend *acknowledge that he is a script reader and not a co-writer*.

STATEMENT BY A READER OF A STORY

I have been asked by writer: — to read a script written by him entitled: — consisting of the following number: — of pages. If any of my comments or possible suggestions are used by WRITER in the future, I will be pleased and I hereby expressly waive any rights I may have arising out of WRITER'S use of my comments or suggestions.

I am signing this on the — day of the month of —, 1972 in the following city: — county: — and state: —.

Signature: —

Name printed:
Street address:
City, state, zip:
Telephone:
Social Security:
State and drivers license number:

QUESTION 27
Should I have statements and contracts notarized?

ANSWER

There is no simple answer. Some documents (real estate, etc.) have to be notarized.

Some people are impressed when their signature is notarized. Sometimes a writing which might be suspected as being a current writing with an old date, is less suspected if there is a notarization containing the old date. Sometimes the inconvenience of getting something notarized (and the expense) outweighs the potential advantages. Write a letter to your state's Secretary of State, % State Capitol, in the capitol of your state. (This may not be the right person to ask in your state.) Ask your information and application form concerning your becoming a notary public. You may find your becoming a notary public (a) a way to be useful and to earn a few dollars, (b) a way to meet people who may have money and to learn about business and real estate, (c) a way to notarize a friendly notary public's personal papers when he needs it, while he notarizes your papers when you need it, (d) a way to get a good looking notary public certificate in your office.

QUESTION 28
How can I find more ready made forms to read, study, and modify so that the modified form fits my purpose?

ANSWER

Some of the books containing forms that others have used for their purposes (which may differ from your purpose and should therefore be modified) are:

1. Alexander Lindey, ENTERTAINMENT PUBLISHING AND THE ARTS AGREEMENTS AND THE LAW.

2. AMERICAN JURISPRUDENCE LEGAL FORMS ANNOTATED.

3. Minus and Hale, THE RECORD INDUSTRY BOOK, THE MOVIE INDUSTRY BOOK, and the other books of THE ENTERTAINMENT INDUSTRY SERIES.

QUESTION 29

I have written a script for myself, and therefore I own the common law copyright. A friend wants me to write a script for him. Who will that common law copyright belong to?

ANSWER

It is a good idea if you and your friend agree on that before you write the script. Here are some possible agreements.

POSSIBILITY NO. 1 — You write the script and it belongs to you. Your friend may use the script to show to potential "money people." At some indefinite time you and your friend may discuss whether or not you still want to give him rights in the script or any other rights, and whether your friend still wants to tie up the rights to make a movie based on your script.

POSSIBILITY NO. 2 — You write the script and it belongs to you. You receive option money (a fraction of the value of the script) and you agree that if within a year (or some other time) your friend pays an option pick up amount (the value of the script), then your friend owns the copyright. If the period of time to exercise the option has passed and your friend has not picked up the option, then you keep both the original option money and the copyright.

POSSIBILITY NO. 3 — Your friend employs you to write the script; he is the employer-for-hire; you are the employee-for-hire. You receive a salary as employee; your work belongs to your employer; the common law copyright belongs to your employer.

POSSIBILITY NO. 4 — You write a script. The common law copyright belongs to you. Your friend wants to use the script to make a school project movie. You license (give permission) to your friend to make one school project movie during the next six months, said movie to be not shown commercially. Your friend says "Thanks." You receive a movie credit. You own the common law copyright to the script and can commercially exploit it any way you can. (Of course, you *may* lose a big movie deal on the script if a potential purchaser learns of the existence of the school movie.)

OTHER POSSIBILITIES — There are many variations of

option agreements, buy-sell-revert agreements, employer-employee agreements, licensing agreements.

In each agreement concerning copyright of anything created by you, see (1) how often you should be paid, (2) how much you will be paid, (3) under what circumstances does the copyright revert to you, (4) what happens if the other party breaks the contract.

QUESTION 30

Who owns the copyright of a student film I make as part of a class assignment? Do I own it, or does the school own it?

ANSWER

If there is a written agreement, see the agreement. If there is no written agreement, worry about the question until there is an argument. There are good agreements for both the school and the individual to claim the copyright. You may prefer to worry about it rather than challenge the school while you are in a weak bargaining position.

There are various film contests and distributors of educational films. You may be able to have your film distributed as a result of winning a contest or because a distributor of educational films is interested. You will be asked to warrant that the copyright in the film belongs to you.

When you make your student film, be sure that you have a proper *copyright notice* on the card bearing the movie title or on the first card thereafter, in the beginning of the film. Most movie makers don't want to "date" their film, and therefore show the year with roman numerals (M=1000, L=100, M=50, X=10, V=5, I=1; MLMXXIV=1974).

CHAPTER 21

COPYRIGHT OFFICE CIRCULARS & FORMS

COPYRIGHT OFFICE

THE LIBRARY OF CONGRESS

WASHINGTON. D.C. 20540

NEW VERSIONS AND REPRINTS

NEW VERSIONS

Under the copyright law (Section 7 of Title 17 of the United States Code) a new version of a work in the public domain, or a new version of a copyrighted work that has been produced by the copyright owner or with his consent, is copyrightable as a "new work." Copyrightable "new works" include compilations, abridgments, adaptations, arrangements, dramatizations, translations, and works republished with new literary, dramatic, musical, pictorial, or sculptural material.

The copyright in a new version covers only the additions, changes, or other new material appearing for the first time in the work. There is no way to restore copyright protection for a work in the public domain, such as by including it in a new version. Likewise, protection for a copyrighted work cannot be lengthened by republishing the work with new matter.

The Copyright Office has no authority to register claims to copyright in mere reprints. To be copyrightable, a new version must either be so different in substance from the original as to be regarded as a "new work," or it must contain an appreciable amount of new material. This new material must be original and copyrightable in itself. When only a few slight variations or minor additions of no substance have been made, or when the revisions or added material consist solely of uncopyrightable elements (for example, titles, short phrases, format, color), registration is not possible.

COMPILATIONS AND ABRIDGMENTS

Any work, to be copyrightable, must be the "writing of an author." Thus, compilations and abridgments may be copyrighted only if their preparation involves authorship. When the assembling of a "compilation" is a purely mechanical task without any element of editorial selection or when the preparation of an "abridgment" involves only a few minor changes or deletions, registration is not possible.

COPYRIGHT NOTICE IN REPRINTS AND NEW VERSIONS

For the copyright in a work to remain in force, it is essential that all published copies contain the correct statutory copyright notice. The form of this notice may vary depending upon the nature of the work. No general rule can cover all possible situations, but the following principles should be considered:

- If the work is a **reprint,** without substantial revisions or new matter, the original copyright notice should be retained. It is especially important to keep the date of the original copyright, since the use of a later date in a reprint would probably invalidate copyright protection altogether. The name of the original copyright owner should be used in the notice, unless an assignment of copyright has been recorded in the Copyright Office. The new owner of a

111

copyright may substitute his name in the notice *after, but not before,* his assignment has been recorded.

- If the work is a *new version*, it may be permissible to use an entirely new notice of copyright, containing the later year date of publication and the name of the owner of copyright in the new version. However, in many cases it may be safer to include copyright notices covering both the old and new material. Example:

© 1962, 1971 John Doe

- If the work contains material which was *originally copyrighted in unpublished form* and is *now published for the first time,* the proper notice depends upon whether or not the original work has been changed. If the published edition is essentially the same as the unpublished version, the notice should contain the year date of original copyright registration. However, if the work as published also contains substantial revisions or new matter, the notice may include either the year date of first publication alone or, preferably, both the year dates of registration and of publication.

May 1971–

COPYRIGHT OFFICE

THE LIBRARY OF CONGRESS

WASHINGTON, D.C. 20540

RENEWAL OF COPYRIGHT

WHAT IS RENEWAL OF COPYRIGHT?

The copyright law (Title 17, U.S. Code, §§ 24, 25) provides that the original term of copyright lasts for 28 years. In the case of a work originally copyrighted in *unpublished* form, this term begins on the date registration was made in the Copyright Office. The copyright term for *published* works begins on the date of first publication. In either case a second 28-year term of copyright may be secured for the work if a valid renewal claim is registered in the Copyright Office within the strict time limits imposed by the law. The second term begins on the date of expiration of the original term, regardless of the date the renewal application is received in the Copyright Office. A renewal claim can be registered only if registration has been made for the first term of copyright in the work.

HOW TO REGISTER A RENEWAL CLAIM

Application for renewal registration should be filed on Form R, which is supplied by the Copyright Office upon request. Each renewal application requires a statutory registration fee of $4, payable to the Register of Copyrights. Where several applications are submitted at the same time, one remittance for the collective amount should be sent. It is not necessary to send copies of the copyrighted work.

TIME LIMITS FOR RENEWAL REGISTRATION

The copyright law prescribes that application for registration of a renewal claim must be made during the last year of the original 28-year term, measured from the exact date on which the original copyright began. For example, if the first term began on May 15, 1943, the copyright would be eligible for renewal between May 15, 1970 and May 15, 1971.

CAUTION: Renewal registration can be made only if an acceptable claim and fee are *received* in the Copyright Office before the end of the first copyright term. If an acceptable application and fee are not received before the original term has expired, the work falls into the public domain and the copyright cannot then be revived. The Copyright Office has no discretion to extend the renewal time limits.

WHO MAY CLAIM RENEWAL?

Renewal copyright may be claimed only by those persons specified in the law.

A. The following persons may claim renewal in all types of works except those enumerated in Paragraph B, below:

    1. The author, if living, may claim as **the author.**

2. If the author is dead, the widow (widower) of the author, or the child (children) of the author, or both, may claim as **the widow (widower) of the author** and/or **the child (children) of the deceased author.**

3. If there is no surviving widow, widower, or child, and the author left a will, his executors may claim as **the executors of the author.**

4. If there is no surviving widow, widower, or child, and the author left no will, the next of kin may claim as **the next of kin of the deceased author, there being no will.**

B. Only in the case of the following four types of works may the copyright proprietor (owner of the copyright at the time of renewal registration) claim renewal:

1. Posthumous work (work first published and copyrighted after the death of the author). Renewal may be claimed as **proprietor of copyright in a posthumous work.**

2. Periodical, cyclopedic, or other composite work. Renewal may be claimed as **proprietor of copyright in a composite work.**

3. Work copyrighted by a corporate body *otherwise than as assignee or licensee of the individual author.* Renewal may be claimed as **proprietor of copyright in a work copyrighted by a corporate body otherwise than as assignee or licensee of the individual author.** (This type of claim is considered appropriate in relatively few cases.)

4. Work copyrighted by an employer for whom such work was made for hire. Renewal may be claimed as **proprietor of copyright in a work made for hire.**

NEW VERSIONS

Copyright in a new version of a previous work (such as an arrangement, translation, dramatization, compilation, or work republished with new matter) covers only the additions, changes, or other new material appearing for the first time in that version. The copyright secured in a new version is independent of any copyright protection in material published earlier, and the only "authors" of a new version are those who contributed copyrightable matter to it. Thus, for renewal purposes, the person who wrote the original version upon which the new work is based cannot be regarded as an "author" of the new version, unless he also contributed to the new matter.

CONTRIBUTIONS TO PERIODICALS OR OTHER COMPOSITE WORKS

Separate renewal registration is possible for a work published as a contribution to a periodical or other composite work, whether the contribution was copyrighted separately or as part of the larger work in which it appeared. In the case of contributions published serially, each separate installment is subject to its own renewal registration, requiring a separate application and fee.

NOTICE OF RENEWAL COPYRIGHT

The Copyright Office is frequently asked whether the notice of copyright should be changed on copies of a work issued during the renewal term. The copyright law is silent on this point, and the continued use of the original form of notice may therefore be considered appropriate. However, a notice which also refers to the fact of renewal might be regarded as more informative and hence preferable; for example:

Copyright 1945 John Doe

Copyright renewed 1973 by Mrs. Mary Doe.

COPYRIGHT OFFICE

THE LIBRARY OF CONGRESS

WASHINGTON, D.C. 20540

TITLES, NAMES, SHORT PHRASES

Names, titles, and short phrases or expressions are not copyrightable. The Copyright Office cannot therefore register claims to exclusive rights in the names of products or organizations, pen names, titles, catchwords, slogans, advertising phrases, mottoes, and the like. This is true even if the name, title, phrase, or expression is novel, distinctive, or lends itself to a play on words.

In order to be copyrightable, a work must contain at least a certain minimum amount of authorship in the form of original literary, artistic, or musical expression. A work deposited for registration in the Copyright Office must have a distinguishing title for purposes of identification, but this does not mean that the title itself is copyrightable. The presence of a title in the Copyright Office registration records does not imply that the title is protected by copyright. Our records contain many instances of different works identified by the same or similar titles.

Some brand names, trade names, slogans, and phrases may be entitled to protection under the general rules of law relating to unfair competition, or to registration under the provisions of the trademark laws. The Copyright Office has no jurisdiction in these matters. Questions about the trademark laws should be addressed to the Commissioner of Patents, U.S. Department of Commerce, Washington, D.C. 20231.

Aug. 1969

INTERNATIONAL
COPYRIGHT
PROTECTION

A. GENERAL INFORMATION ABOUT INTERNATIONAL COPYRIGHT PROTECTION

Sources of Protection in Other Countries

There is no such thing as an "international copyright" that will automatically protect an author's writings throughout the entire world. Protection against unauthorized use in a particular country depends basically on the national laws of that country. However, most countries do offer protection to foreign works under certain conditions, and these conditions have been greatly simplified by international copyright treaties and conventions.

An author who wishes to copyright his work in a particular country should first find out the extent of protection for foreign works in that country. If possible he should do this before his work is published anywhere, since protection may often depend on the facts existing at the time of first publication.

If the country in which protection is sought is a party to one of the international copyright conventions discussed below, the work may generally be protected by complying with the conditions of the convention. Even if the work cannot be brought under an international convention, protection under the specific provisions of the country's national laws may still be possible. There are, however, some countries that offer little or no copyright protection for foreign works under any circumstances.

The Universal Copyright Convention

The Universal Copyright Convention (the UCC) is an international treaty to which the United States is a party. The UCC came into force on September 16, 1955, and as of July 1, 1970, some 58 countries had adhered to it. Its practical purpose is to reduce to a minimum the formalities required for securing copyright among participating countries.

As a general rule, the UCC requires a participating country to give the same protection to foreign works that meet the Convention requirements as it gives to its own domestic works. To qualify for protection under the Convention, a work must have been written by a national of a participating country, or must have been published for the first time in a participating country.

The "Berne" Conventions

The Berne Convention of 1886 and its four revisions (Paris, 1896; Berlin, 1908; Rome, 1928; Brussels, 1948) have established the International Union for the Protection of Literary and Artistic Works, better known as the Berne Union. The latest revision, signed at Stockholm on July 14, 1967, will come into effect when five countries have ratified or acceded to it. As of July 1, 1970, some 60 countries, not including the United States, have adhered to one or more of these conventions and are therefore members of the Berne Union. Protection under these conventions is extended without formalities to works by nationals of any country on the sole condition that first publication take place in a country that belongs to the Berne Union.

The Pan-American Conventions

Western Hemisphere copyright relations are governed to some extent by a series of seven Pan-American Conventions. Among these, the Buenos Aires Convention of 1910 has been ratified by the United States and 17 Latin American nations. It specifies that authors of any contracting country who have secured copyright in their own country will enjoy in each of the other countries the rights it accords its own works, if the work contains "a statement indicating the reservation of the property right."

Bilateral Arrangements and National Laws

In addition to the multilateral copyright conventions discussed above, there are some bilateral treaties or similar arrangements governing the copyright relations of two countries between themselves. Some countries also have laws granting protection to foreign works under certain conditions without regard to any international conventions or treaties. In all of these cases the extent of protection and the requirements for securing copyright vary from country to country.

119

B. UNITED STATES COPYRIGHT PROTECTION FOR FOREIGN WORKS

U.S. Copyright Under the Universal Copyright Convention

● *Eligibility for U.S. copyright under the UCC.* In general, a work is eligible for United States copyright protection under the Universal Copyright Convention if the author is a citizen of a country that is a party to the UCC, or if the work was first published in a UCC country. However, the special UCC exemptions from the registration and manufacturing requirements do not apply to works by U.S. citizens or domiciliaries or to works first published in the United States.

● *The UCC copyright notice.* In order for the work to secure copyright in the United States and to be exempted from registration and manufacturing formalities, all copies must bear the copyright notice prescribed by the Universal Copyright Convention from the time of their first publication. This notice consists of the symbol © accompanied by the name of the copyright owner and the year date of publication. For example: © John Doe 1971.
The notice must be located on the work in such manner and location as to give reasonable notice of the copyright claim.

● *Registration for works protected under the UCC.* A work that qualifies for U.S. copyright under the Universal Copyright Convention secures protection automatically upon publication with a UCC notice. Registration in the Copyright Office is not required during the first 28-year copyright term. However, although registration is optional, it has advantages in some cases:

- ◆ The copyright owner receives a certificate of registration, which is a document needed for bringing suit for infringement in the United States.
- ◆ Registration provides a permanent public record that makes business transactions in the United States easier.
- ◆ No registration fee is required for foreign works if application is made within 6 months after first publication.
- ◆ The facts of registration are included in official catalogs and given wide distribution in the United States and other countries.
- ◆ Registration for the original term will help in renewing the copyright for the second 28-year term, for which registration will still be necessary.

● *UCC exemption from manufacturing requirements.* Works that qualify for U.S. copyright under the UCC do not need to be manufactured in the United States, and may be imported in unlimited quantities. They secure full-term protection from the time of first publication abroad.

U.S. Copyright for Foreign Works Not Qualifying Under the Universal Copyright Convention

Even if a foreign work fails to qualify for UCC protection in the United States, it may still be eligible to secure copyright under other provisions of the U.S. statute. The special UCC exemptions would not be available in such cases, however, and the manufacturing requirements would be applicable. English-language books and periodicals that are manufactured outside the United States and that are not eligible for the UCC exemptions may still secure ad interim copyright, a special form of short-term protection. For further information about ad interim copyright, write to the U.S. Copyright Office for Circular 69.

C. COPYRIGHT PROTECTION IN OTHER COUNTRIES FOR UNITED STATES WORKS

Protection for U.S. Works Under the Universal Copyright Convention

It is possible for a work by a U.S. author to be published in such a way that it secures copyright protection in the United States and, at the same time, in the other countries that are parties to the Universal Copyright Convention. For this result to be accomplished, all published copies of the work must bear a copyright notice that satisfies both the notice provisions of the UCC, discussed in paragraph 2, page 3, and also the notice requirements of the U.S. law.

The copyright notice must consist of the symbol © accompanied by the name of the copyright owner and the year date of publication. For a book or other publication printed in book form, the copyright notice must appear upon the title page or page immediately following. The "page immediately following" is normally the reverse side of the page bearing the title. For a periodical, the notice must appear on the title page, on the first page of text, or under the title heading. For a musical work, the notice must appear either on the title page or on the first page of music.

A special problem arises with respect to the date in the notice for works that are first registered in unpublished form and later published without any substantial changes or added material. The U.S. law requires the notice to contain the year of registration, but the UCC speaks of the "year date of publication." One way to satisfy both requirements is to use two notices; for example:

Copyright 1968 in U.S.A. by John Doe
© under UCC 1971 by John Doe.

Works by U.S. authors, though protected in other countries under the Universal Copyright Convention, do not enjoy the special UCC exemptions from the requirements of the U.S. copyright law. Thus, following publication of the work, the claim to U.S. copyright should be registered in the Copyright Office in the usual way.

Books and periodicals by U.S. citizens and domiciliaries are still subject to the requirement that they be manufactured in the United States in order to be protected for the full term under U.S. law. However, a special five-year "ad interim" copyright is available for English-language books and periodicals that have been manufactured and first published abroad. Ad interim copyright is secured by registration within 6 months of first publication abroad and permits the importation of up to 1,500 copies of the foreign edition.

Protection Other Than the UCC for U.S. Works

The United States is a party to the Buenos Aires Convention of 1910 and, as explained in paragraph 3, page 2, works by U.S. authors nay be protected in the other member countries if the published copies contain a statement that copyright is reserved. Protection for U.S. works in countries that are members of the Berne Union can be obtained by first or simultaneous publication in a Union country, although difficult legal questions can arise as to what constitutes a genuine "first" or "simultaneous" publication in a particular case. In order to be protected in some countries it may be necessary for an American author to comply with specific statutory requirements or administrative regulations, which vary from country to country.

D. APPLICATION FORMS

There are no forms to be filed in the U.S. Copyright Office for copyright in other countries.

The following forms are provided by the Copyright Office for registration of claims to United States copyright, and may be obtained free of charge on request.

Class A Form A—Published book manufactured in the United States of America.

Class A or B
- Form A–B Foreign—Book or periodical manufactured outside the United States of America (except works subject to the ad interim provisions of the copyright law).
- Form A–B Ad Interim—Book or periodical in the English language manufactured and first published outside the United States of America.

Class B
- Form B—Periodical manufactured in the United States of America.
- Form BB—Contribution to a periodical manufactured in the United States of America.

Class C Form C—Lecture or similar production prepared for oral delivery.

Class D Form D—Dramatic or dramatico-musical composition.

Class E
- Form E—Musical composition the author of which is a citizen or domiciliary of the United States of America or which was first published in the United States of America.
- Form E Foreign—Musical composition the author of which is not a citizen or domiciliary of the United States of America and which was not first published in the United States of America.

Class F Form F—Map.

Class G Form G—Work of art or a model or design for a work of art.

Class H Form H—Reproduction of a work of art.

Class I Form I—Drawing or plastic work of a scientific or technical character.

Class J Form J—Photograph.

Class K
- Form K—Print or pictorial illustration.
- Form KK—Print or label used for an article of merchandise.

Class L
or M } Form L–M—Motion picture.

Form R—Renewal copyright.

Form U—Notice of use of copyrighted music on mechanical instruments.

E. MAIL AND REMITTANCES

Address. All mail to the U.S. Copyright Office should be addressed to the Register of Copyrights, Library of Congress, Washington, D.C. 20540, U.S.A.

Remittance. All fees sent to the Copyright Office should be payable in U.S. funds and should be in the form of a money order, check, or bank draft payable to the *Register of Copyrights*.

Mailing. Processing of the material will be more prompt if the application, copies, and fee are all mailed at the same time and in the same package.

F. INFORMATION FURNISHED

This circular attempts to answer some of the questions that the Copyright Office is most commonly asked about international copyright matters. The Office also furnishes on request current lists of the copyright relations of various countries (Circulars 38A, 38B, and 38C) and a variety of circulars dealing with the U.S. copyright law. Specific questions concerning the method of securing and registering U.S. copyright protection should be addressed to the Register of Copyrights, Library of Congress, Washington, D.C. 20540, U.S.A.

For current information on the requirements and protection provided by other countries, it may be advisable to consult an expert familiar with foreign copyright laws. The U.S. Copyright Office is not permitted to recommend agents or attorneys or to give legal advice or information on foreign laws.

U.S. GOVERNMENT PRINTING OFFICE: 1971   O—411–547

INTERNATIONAL COPYRIGHT RELATIONS OF THE UNITED STATES

(As of February 1, 1971)

Code:		
UCC	Party to the Universal Copyright Convention, as is the United States. The effective date is given for each country. The effective date for the United States was September 16, 1955.
BAC	Party to the Buenos Aires Convention of 1910, as is the United States.
Bilateral	Bilateral copyright relations with the United States by virtue of a proclamation or treaty.
Unclear	Became independent since 1943. Has not established copyright relations with the United States, but may be honoring obligations incurred under former political status.
None	No copyright relations with the United States.

Country   **Status of Copyright Relations**

Country	Status of Copyright Relations
Afghanistan	None
Albania	None
Algeria	Unclear
Andorra	UCC Sept. 16, 1955
Argentina	UCC Feb. 13, 1958, BAC, Bilateral
Australia	UCC May 1, 1969, Bilateral
Austria	UCC July 2, 1957, Bilateral
Barbados	Unclear
Belgium	UCC Aug. 31, 1960, Bilateral
Bhutan	None

125

Country	Status
Bolivia	BA
Botswana	Uncle
Brazil	UCC Jan. 13, 1960, BAC, Bilater
Bulgaria	No■
Burma	Uncle
Burundi	Uncle
Cambodia	UCC Sept. 16, 19!
Cameroon	Uncle
Canada	UCC Aug. 10, 1962, Bilater
Central African Republic	Uncle
Ceylon	Uncle
Chad	Uncle
Chile	UCC Sept. 16, 1955, BAC, Bilater
China	Bilater
Colombia	BA
Congo (Brazzaville)	Uncle
Congo (Kinshasa)	Uncle
Costa Rica	UCC Sept. 16, 1955, BAC, Bilater
Cuba	UCC Sept. 18, 1957, Bilater
Cyprus	Uncle
Czechoslovakia	UCC Jan. 6, 1960, Bilater
Dahomey	Uncle
Denmark	UCC Feb. 9, 1962, Bilater
Dominican Republic	BA
Ecuador	UCC June 5, 1957, BA
El Salvador	Bilateral by virtue of Mexico City Convention, 19■
Equatorial Guinea	Uncle
Ethiopia	No■
Fiji	Uncle
Finland	UCC April 16, 1963, Bilate■
France	UCC Jan. 14, 1956, Bilate■
Gabon	Uncle
Gambia	Uncle
Germany	Bilateral, UCC with Federal Republic of Germany, Sept. 16, 19■
Ghana	UCC Aug. 22, 19■
Greece	UCC Aug. 24, 1963, Bilate.
Guatemala	UCC Oct. 28, 1964, BA
Guinea	Uncle

yana . . . . Unclear

iti . . . . UCC Sept. 16, 1955, BAC

ly See . . . . UCC Oct. 5, 1955

nduras . . . . BAC

ngary . . . . UCC Jan. 23, 1971, Bilateral

land . . . . UCC Dec. 18, 1956

lia . . . . UCC Jan. 21, 1958, Bilateral

lonesia . . . . Unclear

n . . . . None

ą . . . . None

land . . . . UCC Jan. 20, 1959, Bilateral

ael . . . . UCC Sept. 16, 1955, Bilateral

.y . . . . UCC Jan. 24, 1957, Bilateral

ry Coast . . . . Unclear

aica . . . . Unclear

an . . . . UCC April 28, 1956

dan . . . . Unclear

nya . . . . UCC Sept. 7, 1966

rea . . . . Unclear

wait . . . . Unclear

s . . . . UCC Sept. 16, 1955

anon . . . . UCC Oct. 17, 1959

otho . . . . Unclear

eria . . . . UCC July 27, 1956

ya . . . . Unclear

chtenstein . . . . UCC Jan. 22, 1959

xembourg . . . . UCC Oct. 15, 1955, Bilateral

dagascar . . . . Unclear

lawi . . . . UCC Oct. 26, 1965

laysia . . . . Unclear

ldive Islands . . . . Unclear

li . . . . Unclear

lta . . . . UCC Nov. 19, 1968

uritania . . . . Unclear

uritius [1] . . . . UCC Mar. 12, 1968

---

[1] On August 20, 1970, Unesco was notified by the Government of Mauritius that it considers itself bound
he UCC from March 12, 1968.

Mexico . . . . UCC May 12, 1957, BAC, Bilate

Monaco . . . . UCC Sept. 16, 1955, Bilate

Morocco . . . . Uncl

Nauru . . . . Uncl

Nepal . . . . Nε

Netherlands . . . . UCC June 22, 1967, Bilate

New Zealand . . . . UCC Sept. 11, 1964, Bilate

Nicaragua . . . . UCC Aug. 16, 1961, B,

Niger . . . . Uncl

Nigeria . . . . UCC Feb. 14, 19

Norway . . . . UCC Jan. 23, 1963, Bilate

Oman . . . . Nε

Pakistan . . . . UCC Sept. 16, 19

Panama . . . . UCC Oct. 17, 1962, B,

Paraguay . . . . UCC Mar. 11, 1962, B,

Peru . . . . UCC Oct. 16, 1963, B

Philippines . . . . Bilateral, UCC status undetermined by UNESℂ

(Copyright Office considers that UCC relations do not exi

Poland . . . . Bilate

Portugal . . . . UCC Dec. 25, 1956, Bilate

Romania . . . . Bilate

Rwanda . . . . Uncl

San Marino . . . . Nε

Saudi Arabia . . . . Nε

Senegal . . . . Uncl

Sierra Leone . . . . Uncl

Singapore . . . . Uncl

Somalia . . . . Uncl

South Africa . . . . Bilate

Soviet Union . . . . Nε

Spain . . . . UCC Sept. 16, 1955, Bilate

Sudan . . . . Uncl

Swaziland . . . . Uncl

Sweden . . . . UCC July 1, 1961, Bilate

Switzerland . . . . UCC March 30, 1956, Bilate

Syria . . . . Uncl

Tanzania . . . . Uncl

Thailand . . . . Bilate

go.. Unclear
nga...None
nidad and Tobago...Unclear
nisia..UCC June 19, 1969
rkey.........................,................................None
anda.. Unclear
ited Arab Republic (Egypt).................................None
ited Kingdom................................UCC Sept. 27, 1957, Bilateral
per Volta..Unclear
uguay..BAC
nezuela...UCC Sept. 30, 1966
tnam..Unclear
estern Samoa..Unclear
men (Aden)...Unclear
men (San'a)...None
goslavia...UCC May 11, 1966
nbia...UCC June 1, 1965

BERNE UNION MEMBER COUNTRIES [2]
(As of January 1, 1971)

The United States is not a member of the Berne Union. The following list is furnish
by the Copyright Office merely as a service for persons interested in the Berne Uni

Argentina	Germany (Fed. Rep.)	Netherlands
Australia	Greece	New Zealand
Austria	Holy See	Niger
Belgium	Hungary	Norway
Brazil	Iceland	Pakistan
Bulgaria	India	Philippines
Cameroon	Ireland	Poland
Canada	Israel	Portugal
Ceylon	Italy	Romania
Chile	Ivory Coast	Senegal
Congo (Brazzaville)	Japan	South Africa
Congo (Kinshasa)	Lebanon	Spain
Cyprus	Liechtenstein	Sweden
Czechoslovakia	Luxembourg	Switzerland
Dahomey	Madagascar	Thailand
Denmark	Mali	Tunisia
Finland	Malta	Turkey
France	Mexico	United Kingdom
Gabon	Monaco	Uruguay
Germany (Dem. Rep.) [3]	Morocco	Yugoslavia

The Berne Convention of 1886 and its four revisions (Paris, 1896; Berlin, 19
Rome, 1928; Brussels, 1948) have established the International Union for the Pro
tion of Literary and Artistic Works, better known as the Berne Union. The count
listed above have adhered to this Convention and are therefore members of the Be
Union. (A fifth revision, signed at Stockholm on July 14, 1967, has not yet come i
force.)

Questions about the operation and provisions of the Berne Convehtion should
sent to the United International Bureaux for the Protection of Intellectual Prop
(BIRPI), 32, chemin des Colombettes (Place des Nations), 1211 Geneva 20, Swit
land, which is responsible for the administration of the Berne Union.

---

[2] Source: "Members of the Berne Union as of January 1, 1971," in *Copyright* (*BIRPI*), vol. 7, no. 1 (Jar
1971), pp. 8–9.

[3] The membership of Germany (Dem. Rep.) is disputed by some members.

COPYRIGHT OFFICE
The Library of Congress
Washington, D.C. 20540

COPYRIGHT FOR MOTION PICTURES

What Is a "Motion Picture"?

In general, the term "motion picture" applies to complete photographic films ready for projection or exhibition. It does not include scenarios or synopses, and the Copyright Office cannot register works of this sort in unpublished form. Filmstrips and slide films are generally registrable as "photographs" on Form J.

The general idea, outline, or title of a motion picture or of a filmed series cannot be copyrighted. Registration of one film does not protect other films in a series or give any sort of "blanket" protection to the series as a whole.

Class of Motion Pictures

The copyright law provides for two classes of motion pictures:

Class L, *motion-picture photoplays*, for motion pictures that are dramatic in character and tell a connected story, such as feature films, filmed television plays, short subjects having a plot, and animated cartoons.

Class M, *motion pictures other than photoplays*, for such films as newsreels, travelogs, training or promotional films, nature studies, and filmed television programs having no plot.

Application forms are furnished free by the Copyright Office upon request. The form for all motion pictures is designated Form L-M.

Published Motion Pictures

Copyright is secured on the date of first publication if all copies distributed bear notice of copyright. "Publication" generally means the sale, placing on sale, or public distribution of copies; in the case of motion pictures it may also include distribution to film exchanges, film distributors, exhibitors, or broadcasters under a lease or similar arrangement.

The copyright notice must consist of the word "Copyright," the abbreviation "Copr.," or the symbol ©, accompanied by the name of the copyright proprietor and the year date of publication. Example:

©John Doe 1969

The notice should preferably appear on the title frame or near it. The use of the symbol © with the name of the copyright owner and the year date may result in securing copyright in countries outside the United States under the provisions of the Universal Copyright Convention.

NOTE: Once a work has been published without the required copyright notice, the right to secure copyright protection for that film is permanently lost.

Promptly *after publication* the following items should be deposited in the Copyright Office:

Two complete copies of the best edition of the motion picture then published. The "best" edition is usually the most valuable form of prints available — for example, color prints rather than black and white, or 35mm. rather than 16mm;

An application on Form L-M. Item 3 of this application *must* be checked to show whether the film is Class L or Class M. If the motion picture is part of a series, the application should list both the series and episode title;

A description in the form of a continuity, press book, etc; and

The stautory registration fee of $6.

The copies (i.e., reels) of published motion pictures deposited in the Copyright Office are subject to retention by the Library of Congress under the provisions of section 213 of the copyright law. A contract, however, may be made with the Librarian for the return to the applicant of the deposited copies under certain conditions. For information regarding this contract, address the Exchange and Gift Division, Library of Congress, Washington, D.C. 20540. Contract forms will be supplied by the Copyright Office upon request.

Unpublished Motion Pictures

Copyright may also be secured for an unpublished motion picture (i.e., one not reproduced in copies for sale or public distribution), upon deposit in the Copyright Office of the following:

One print (i.e., frame or blow-up) taken from each scene or act if the film is a photoplay, *or* at least two prints taken from different sections if the film is not a photoplay;

An application on Form L-M. Item 3 of the application

must be checked to show whether the film is Class L or Class M;

The title and description of the film in the form of a continuity, press book, etc.; and

The statutory registration fee of $6.

Registration of a claim prior to publication does not relieve the claimant of the duty of depositing, with an application and registration fee, two copies of the best edition of the published film after copies containing the stautory copyright notice have been placed on sale, sold, or publicly distributed.

A complete play with dialog and dramatic action, ready for filming, may be registered as a "dramatic composition." Ask for application Form D.

Jan. 1971

Announcement

from the Copyright Office, Library of Congress, Washington, D.C. 20540

CHANGES IN COPYRIGHT OFFICE REGULATIONS

Section 202.15 of the Regulations of the Copyright Office (Chapter II of Title 37 of the Code of Federal Regulations), which relates to the registration of motion pictures, has been amended by adding the following provisions, which appeared in the May 14, 1971, issue of the FEDERAL REGISTER, Volume 36, Number 94, at page 8869.

Title 37—PATENTS, TRADE-MARKS, AND COPYRIGHTS

Chapter II—Copyright Office, Library of Congress

PART 202—REGISTRATION OF CLAIMS TO COPYRIGHT

Deposit for Registration of Motion Pictures

Section 202.15 of Chapter II of Title of the Code of Federal Regulations amended by adding new paragraphs) and (d) reading as follows:

202.15 Motion pictures (Classes L–M).

* * * * *

(c) *Deposit copies of motion pictures.* the case of published motion pictures bmitted for registration in Classes L M, the requirement for deposit of wo complete copies of the best edition ereof then published" will be satisfied the deposit of identical copies of that ition of the motion picture, from hong any two or more editions in ex-ence, that in the opinion of the Reg-er of Copyrights most closely conforms the established criteria of the Library Congress with respect to the acquisi-n and retention of copies of motion tures for its collections, as expressed the Library of Congress acquisitions licy statement in effect at the time of e deposit. The Copyright Office will rnish to any person concerned, upon request, a copy of the pertinent Library of Congress acquisitions policy statement then in effect.

(d) *Videotape copies.* If otherwise qualified as a motion picture, a work published in the form of videotape copies may be registered in Class L or M. If a motion picture is published in both video-tape and film copies, the requirement for deposit of "two complete copies of the best edition thereof then published" will be satisfied by the deposit of two identical film copies in accordance with paragraph (c) of this section. If a mo-tion picture is published solely in the form of videotape copies, the deposit re-quirement will be satisfied by the deposit of two identical videotape copies accom-panied by a set of photographic repro-ductions of portions of the videotape copies showing the title of the work, the copyright notice, the production, per-formance and other creativity credits, and two or more scenes from different sections of the work.

(Sec. 207, 61 Stat. 666; 17 U.S.C. 207)

Effective date. This amendment shall become effective on the date of its publication in the FEDERAL REGISTER (5–14–71).

ABRAHAM L. KAMINSTEIN,
Register of Copyrights.

Approved:

L. QUINCY MUMFORD,
Librarian of Congress.

[FR Doc.71-6710 Filed 5-13-71; 8:46 am]

L 73
ne 1971--4,000

Extract from Library of Congress
Acquisitions Policy Statement
on Motion Pictures
(as of August 15, 1971)

Section V. Form of Copies

When a motion picture is available in more than one edition, the Library will seek to acquire the most complete, uncut, and authentic edition available. As to the form of the copies, the Library generally prefers, and will select or try to acquire the following:

— Copies reproduced on either 35 mm. or 16 mm. film, if available, the preference depending on which gauge represents the form in which copies of the work are most widely distributed for public exhibition. The Library's general preference as to size is not affected by the existence of copies in any larger or smaller size or of copies that have been reproduced by a process requiring special or unconventional forms of projection. Where copies have been issued in the form of video tape, the Library still prefers to receive a film transfer if available.

— Copies reproduced in color, if readily available in the size preferred by the Library, rather than in monochrome.

— Copies accompanied by sound, where both sound and silent versions are available; where versions exist in different languages, the Library prefers the original language version, but will also attempt to acquire, when needed, the English version.

— Where copies exist only in the form of video tape, copies reproduced on 2-inch tape, if available.

Exceptions to the above policies will be made under the following conditions:

1. If the motion picture has been produced by a new process or a unique combination of processes, if it exists in a new or unique format, or if the copies require a new or unique method for their showing, the Library prefers to acquire copies reflecting the new or unique process, format, or method. Where the copies in such a case are copyright deposits, the Head of the Motion Picture Section of the Prints and Photographs Division will notify the Head of the Arts Section in the Examining Division, Copyright Office, that an exception should be made.

2. Where the person depositing for copyright registration proposes to submit copies that do not satisfy the general acquisitions policies outlined above, the Copyright Office will consult the Head of the Motion Picture Section who may, after weighing the factors, recommend that an exception be made for one or more works.

3. Where the person depositing for copyright registration proposes to submit copies that, although satisfying the general acquisitions policies outlined above, are different in form from the copy of the particular work that the Library wishes to retain for its collections, the Copyright Office will consult the Head of the Motion Picture Section. The latter may, after weighing the factors, recommend that the deposit copies be accepted for copyright registration only on condition that the claimant bind himself under a Supplemental Motion Picture Agreement to deliver on demand a copy of a different description.

COPYRIGHT OFFICE

THE LIBRARY OF CONGRESS

WASHINGTON, D.C. 20540

———

RADIO AND TELEVISION PROGRAMS

WHAT *CANNOT* BE COPYRIGHTED

● *Ideas and Titles.* The general idea or title of a radio or television program cannot be copyrighted. In some circumstances it may be possible for titles and ideas to be protected by means of a contract or under state laws of unfair competition, but this has nothing to do with copyright. Copyright registration protects only the material deposited in this Office. Registration for a single script covers the copyrightable material in that script, but does not give any sort of "blanket" protection to future scripts, to a series as a whole, or to any other material that is not actually a part of the copy deposited.

● *Unpublished Synopses.* To be acceptable for copyright registration in unpublished form, a script must be more than an outline or synopsis. It should be ready for presentation or performance, so that a program could actually be produced from the script deposited.

WHAT CAN BE COPYRIGHTED

● *Scripts.* The unpublished script for a radio or television program, or a group of related scripts comprising a series, may ordinarily be registered for copyright. The application should be submitted on Form C if the script is nondramatic (such as a lecture, panel discussion, or variety program). Form D should be used if the work is in the form of a play, musical comedy, shooting script of a screenplay, or similar "dramatic composition." In the case of a series of related programs, each separate script should contain a different episode number or issue date to distinguish it from the others.

● *Filmed Television Programs.* A television program or commercial may be copyrighted as a motion picture. The application for registration should be submitted on Form L–M. Class L (motion-picture photoplays) includes dramatic motion pictures such as features, serials, animated cartoons, musical plays, and similar works. Class M (motion pictures other than photoplays) includes nondramatic motion pictures such as newsreels, musical shorts, travelogs, educational films, and works of a similar nature.

● *Other Elements of a Program.* In addition to scripts and motion pictures, various other parts of a radio or television program may be registered under one of the specific classes provided in the copyright law. For example, musical compositions may be registered in Class E, works of art in Class G, photographs in Class J, etc. Sound recordings are not accepted as deposit copies, and should not be sent to the Copyright Office.

Copyrightable material embodied in a radio or television commercial, such as a script or musical composition, may be registered in the Copyright Office. Phrases, slogans, or other short

139

expressions are not copyrightable. Form C may be filed for a narrated commercial, Form D for one in dramatic form, and Form E for a musical composition.

● *Published Works.* To secure and maintain copyright in a published work, all copies must bear the statutory copyright notice in the prescribed form and position. Example: © John Doe 1971. Publication is generally regarded as the sale, placing on sale, or public distribution of copies of the work.

Application forms and circulars describing the statutory notice and registration requirements may be obtained from the Copyright Office free of charge upon request.

GPO:1971—O—438—650

Sept. 1971—10,000

COPYRIGHT OFFICE

THE LIBRARY OF CONGRESS

WASHINGTON, D.C. 20540

RADIO AND TELEVISION PROGRAMS

Because there are so many misconceptions about copyright registration for radio and television material, we should like to emphasize the following general points:

● The title of a program, as such, cannot be protected by copyright.

● The general idea or outline for a program is not copyrightable. Copyright will protect the literary or dramatic expression of an author's ideas, but not the ideas themselves.

● Registration for a particular script covers the copyrightable material in that script, but does not give "blanket" protection to future scripts or to a series as a whole.

Each separate script for a series of related programs should contain a different episode number or issue date to distinguish it from the others.

February 1971

COPYRIGHT OFFICE

THE LIBRARY OF CONGRESS

WASHINGTON. D.C. 20540

DRAMATICO-MUSICAL WORKS

WHAT IS A "DRAMATICO-MUSICAL COMPOSITION"

Operas, music dramas, musical comedies, musical plays for television, and other productions in which music and drama are integrated are classified as "dramatico-musical compositions" registrable in Class D.

UNPUBLISHED DRAMATICO-MUSICAL WORKS

A dramatico-musical work can be registered for copyright in unpublished form, either as a complete entity or in separate parts consisting of the script for the dramatic portions and the score for the music. These alternatives are described in more detail below. The work as deposited for registration must be developed to the point from which it can be presented in dramatic form. An unpublished outline or synopsis of a dramatico-musical work cannot be registered for copyright.

Unpublished works may be registered by depositing a complete copy of the particular work to be registered, an application on Form D, and a fee of $6. Tape recordings and other sound recordings are not acceptable as deposits. An application and fee are required for each separate registration, though the registration fees covering several applications submitted at the same time can be combined in a single check or money order.

NOTE: When a work has been registered in unpublished form, a second registration is generally required after the work has been published. The "date of publication" is defined as the earliest date on which copies are placed on sale, sold, or publicly distributed by authority of the copyright proprietor. The broadcast, performance, or recording of a work is not regarded as publication.

PUBLISHED DRAMATICO-MUSICAL WORKS

When a dramatico-musical composition, or any part of it, is published, it is essential that all copies contain the required statutory copyright notice. Copyright protection for a published work can be secured and maintained only if every published copy contains a notice in the correct form and position. If the notice is omitted from the published copies of the work, protection is lost permanently.

For dramatico-musical works the notice should consist of the word "Copyright," the abbreviation "Copr.," or the symbol ©, accompanied by the name of the copyright owner and the year date of publication. Example:

© John Doe 1971

Using the symbol © may secure some additional protection in countries belonging to the Universal Copyright Convention.

For dramatico-musical works the law requires that the notice appear on the "title page or page immediately following." The required location for musical works is the "title page or first page of music." Thus, if parts of a musical score are published separately, as songs or otherwise, the safest location for the notice is the title page of the copies as published.

Promptly after publication, registration for a work published with copyright notice should be made in the Copyright Office. You should send the Office two copies of the best edition as published. They should be accompanied by a fee of $6 and the appropriate application form.

HOW TO DETERMINE WHICH APPLICATION FORM TO USE

- **Dramatico-musical work as a whole.** For a complete dramatico-musical composition, including the script of the dramatic portions (i.e., the libretto, "book," or play), the song lyrics, if separate from the script, and the musical score, use Form D.

- **Dramatic parts alone.** Also use Form D for registration of the script of the dramatic parts without the music.

- **Music alone.** For the complete musical score of a dramatico-musical work, without any words, use Form E. If the music is accompanied by the words of the libretto or by song lyrics that convey the dramatic content of the work, Form D may be more appropriate. However, for separate registrations of individual songs or instrumental compositions taken from the score, use a separate Form E for each.

- **Pictorial and graphic works.** Use Form G for scenery sketches, costume drawings, or other pictorial or artistic works produced in connection with the dramatico-musical work. Material of this sort cannot be included as part of the registration in Class D for an unpublished dramatico-musical composition as a whole.

- **Choreography.** A choreographic work can be registered in Class D on Form D if it conveys a dramatic concept or idea and if it is complete enough for performance without further development. The particular movements and physical actions of which the dance consists must be fixed in some sort of legible written form, such as detailed verbal descriptions, dance notation, pictorial or graphic diagrams, or a combination of these.

Application forms are furnished without charge by the Copyright Office, on request for a particular kind and quantity.

May 1972–

145

COPYRIGHT OFFICE

THE LIBRARY OF CONGRESS

WASHINGTON, D.C. 20540

SYNOPSES, FORMATS, AND OUTLINES

UNPUBLISHED SYNOPSES NOT REGISTRABLE

Narrative outlines, formats, plot summaries of plays and motion pictures, skeletal librettos, and other synopses and outlines cannot be registered for copyright in unpublished form. They are considered "books" under the copyright law, and a "book" cannot be registered unless it has been published with the required copyright notice. As long as they remain unpublished, books are protected against unauthorized use, without either the need or the possibility of registration in the Copyright Office.

IDEAS AND PLANS NOT COPYRIGHTABLE

Copyright protects only the particular manner of expression an author uses in working out his ideas or plans in literary, dramatic, musical, or artistic form. It does not protect any of the ideas or plans on which the author bases his work, or which he embodies in it. Therefore, it is not possible to register a claim to copyright in the idea for a motion picture, television program, story, or any other kind of work.

WORKS REGISTRABLE FOR COPYRIGHT

In some cases copyright registration can be made if an outline or synopsis is developed into a finished work:

- *Dramatic Compositions.* The copyright law provides for the registration of "dramatic compositions" in either published or unpublished form. Plays, operas, musical comedies, shooting scripts or photoplays, television plays, and ballets or pantomimes in written dramatic form can be submitted for registration with Form D. To be considered a "dramatic composition" a work must be ready for performance without the need for developing it any further. It must tell its story by means of dialog or dramatic action rather than narrative or description. An outline, synopsis, or story capable of being dramatized later is not considered a "dramatic composition."

147

- *Scripts of Lectures, Variety Programs, etc.* Form C is used for scripts of works such as lectures, speeches, nondramatic monologs and commercial messages, panel discussions, and variety programs prepared for radio or television. If these are deposited in a form ready for presentation, and not as an outline or synopsis, they can be registered as unpublished works. Tapes or other sound recordings are not acceptable as deposit copies.

- *Motion Pictures.* The copyright law also provides for registration of published and unpublished motion pictures. The term "motion picture" applies to complete photographic films or video tapes ready for projection or exhibition. Form L–M is used for registration of a claim to copyright in a motion picture.

COPYRIGHT FOR PUBLISHED WORKS

A synopsis or outline, if published with copyright notice, can usually be registered as a "book" on Form A. However, as explained above, protection would be limited to the particular literary expression the author used in preparing the synopsis or outline itself, and would not extend to the ideas or plans.

Publication, for copyright purposes, is generally regarded as the sale, placing on sale, or public distribution of authorized copies of a work. To secure and maintain copyright protection for any type of work, the owner of the work must make sure that all copies contain the prescribed copyright notice from the time of first publication. Publication of a work without the required notice will destroy copyright protection permanently.

148

The copyright notice generally consists of the word "Copyright," the abbreviation "Copr.," or the symbol ©, accompanied by the name of the copyright owner and the year date of publication. For example:

© John Doe 1972

The specific notice requirements vary from class to class, but for published dramatic works and scripts the notice must appear on the title page or page immediately following. For further information, request Circular 3.

Registration for a work published with notice of copyright is generally required, even if the work has already been registered for copyright in unpublished form.

APPLICATION FORMS

Application forms, which are furnished by the Copyright Office on request, contain instructions for securing copyright registration. In requesting forms, please specify the particular kind and quantity desired.

Aug. 1972—

Copyright

for

Musical Compositions

GENERAL INFORMATION

WHAT IS A MUSICAL COMPOSITION? The copyright law of the United States (Title 17, U.S.C.) provides for copyright in "musical compositions." This term includes original compositions consisting of music alone or of words and music combined. It also includes arrangements and other new versions of earlier compositions if new copyrightable work of authorship has been added. The term "musical compositions" *does not include song poems or other works consisting of words without music.*

OWNER'S RIGHTS. The owner of a copyrighted musical composition has certain exclusive rights in his work. These include the right to publish copies, the right to make new arrangements or other versions of the composition (which can also be copyrighted), the right to perform it in public for profit, and (subject to certain restrictions) the right to make sound recordings of it. Our circular describing the important requirements for *notice of use of copyrighted music on sound recordings* may be obtained upon request.

DURATION OF COPYRIGHT. Copyright normally begins on the date the work is first published, but, if the work is registered for copyright in unpublished form, copyright protection begins on the date registration is made. In either case, copyright lasts for 28 years from the exact date it begins and is subject to renewal for a second term of 28 years. The requirements and time limits for renewal registration are explained in Circular 15, which may be obtained upon request.

ACCEPTABLE DEPOSIT COPIES. For purposes of deposit in the Copyright Office, the musical composition should be written in some form of legible notation. If the composition includes words, they should if possible be written beneath the notes to which they are sung.

A "lead sheet" is acceptable as the deposit copy for an *unpublished* work, but it is important to realize that copyright registration in that case extends only to the material contained in the deposit copy. If there is a more complete version for which protection is desired, the complete version should be deposited. "Lead sheets" may also be deposited for copyright registration covering a *published* work if they represent complete copies of the best edition as first published.

Phonograph records, tape recordings, and other sound recordings are not regarded as "copies" of the musical compositions reproduced on them. The Copyright Office therefore does not accept recordings for deposit, and they should not be sent to this Office.

HOW TO COPYRIGHT A MUSICAL COMPOSITION

COPYRIGHTS NOT GRANTED BY COPYRIGHT OFFICE. The Copyright Office registers claims to copyrights and issues certificates of registration, but it does not "grant" or "issue" copyrights. Statutory copyright protection is the protection afforded by the Federal law when certain requirements are met. It is secured by the claimant himself, by following one of the methods explained below.

METHODS FOR SECURING COPYRIGHT. There are basically two ways to secure statutory copyright in a musical composition: (1) By registering it in the Copyright Office in unpublished form, or (2) by publishing the work with the statutory notice of copyright affixed to each copy. The procedures to be followed in each case are outlined on pages 3 and 4 of this circular.

UNPUBLISHED MUSICAL COMPOSITIONS

HOW TO REGISTER A CLAIM. To obtain copyright registration for an unpublished musical composition, send the following material, together, to the Copyright Office, Library of Congress, Washington, D.C. 20540:

> *Application Form E.* This form is provided by the Copyright Office, and may be obtained free upon request. It should be properly completed and signed.

> *Copy.* Send one complete copy of the musical composition. Because manuscripts are not returned, do not send your only copy.

> *Fee.* The registration fee is $6. Make the check or money order payable to the Register of Copyrights. Currency is sent at the remitter's risk.

After registration, the Copyright Office issues a certificate as evidence that the claim has been registered. Once a certificate has been issued, no further action in the Copyright Office is necessary until the work has been published, recorded, or substantially revised. Information about copyright for published works appears on page 4 of this circular; for information about what to do when a work is recorded, write for Circular 5, and for information about copyright for revised works, write for Circular 35B.

IS REGISTRATION NECESSARY? Copyright registration for an unpublished musical composition is not required in order to protect the work. Unpublished works are ordinarily protected automatically against unauthorized use by the "common law" of the various States. On the other hand, registration in the Copyright Office for an unpublished musical composition has certain advantages, and may sometimes be important, especially if a sound recording is to be made.

WORDS ALONE NOT REGISTRABLE. Song lyrics without music are not registrable for copyright in unpublished form.

152

PUBLISHED MUSICAL COMPOSITIONS

WHAT IS "PUBLICATION"? Publication generally means the sale, placing on sale, or public distribution of copies. Performance of the work or the making of sound recordings does not constitute publication. While the sale or public distribution of recordings may affect common law rights in the musical composition on the record, it is not regarded as the kind of "publication" that will secure a statutory copyright. Limited distribution of so-called "professional" copies to publishers, bandleaders, etc., ordinarily would not constitute publication. However, the dividing line between a preliminary distribution and actual publication may sometimes be difficult to determine. The author may wish to affix notice of copyright to copies that are to be circulated beyond his control, to show that his interests in the work are reserved.

COPYRIGHT NOTICE REQUIRED FOR PUBLISHED COMPOSITIONS. Even if the work has already been registered for copyright in unpublished form, the following three steps must be taken to preserve copyright protection in the published composition:

- *Produce copies with copyright notice.* Produce the work in copies by printing or other means of reproduction. Make sure that every copy contains a copyright notice in the correct form and position, as explained on page 5.
- *Publish the work with copyright notice.* Place the copies on sale, sell, or publicly distribute them.
- *Register the copyright claim.* Promptly *after* publication, send the following material, together, to the Copyright Office, Library of Congress, Washington, D.C. 20540:

  APPLICATION FORM E. This form is provided by the Copyright Office, and may be obtained free upon request. It should be properly completed and signed.

  COPIES. Send two complete copies of the best edition of the composition as first published with the notice of copyright.

  FEE. The registration fee is $6. Make the check or money order payable to the Register of Copyrights. Currency is sent at the remitter's risk.

153

COPYRIGHT PROCEDURE FOR PUBLISHED MUSICAL COMPOSITIONS. In order to secure and maintain copyright protection for a published composition, it is essential that all published copies contain the required statutory copyright notice. The person entitled to the copyright may place the copyright notice in his work without obtaining permission from the Copyright Office.

THE COPYRIGHT NOTICE

ELEMENTS OF THE NOTICE. The notice must contain these three elements:

- *The word "Copyright," or the abbreviation "Copr.," or the symbol* ©. Use of the symbol © may result in securing copyright in some countries outside the United States under the provisions of the Universal Copyright Convention. See page 7.
- *The year date of publication.* This is ordinarily the year in which copies of the work are first placed on sale, sold, or publicly distributed by the copyright proprietor or under his authority. However, if the work has previously been registered for copyright in unpublished form, the notice should contain the year date of registration for the unpublished version. Or, if there is new copyrightable matter in the published version, it is advisable to include both the year date of registration as an unpublished work and the year date of publication.
- *The name of the copyright owner (or owners).*

FORM OF THE NOTICE. The three elements must be legible, and must appear together, for example:

© John Doe 1968

POSITION OF THE NOTICE. The notice must appear upon the title page or the first page of music.

> **NOTE:** If the work is published without the required notice, copyright is lost and cannot be restored. Adding the correct notice later will not restore protection or permit the Copyright Office to register a claim.

COLLECTIONS OF MUSIC

UNPUBLISHED COLLECTIONS. Generally, a separate application, copy, and fee should be submitted for each separate musical composition to be registered. However, it is possible to register two or more unpublished compositions as a "collection," with one application and fee, when **all** of the following conditions are met:

○ The collection is assembled in an orderly form;
○ The collection bears a single title identifying the collection as a whole;
○ The collection as a whole is the subject of a single claim of copyright; and
○ All the compositions (or arrangements) are by the same author; or if they are by different authors, the collection as a whole represents the work of a single author in its compilation or editing.

The Copyright Office catalogs and indexes covering a single registration for a collection of music will show only the collective title. In order to have the individual compositions cataloged and indexed under their separate titles, it is necessary to register them separately.

Where the collection consists entirely of previously published or registered music and the copyright claim is limited to the compilation, the work can be regarded as a "book" for copyright purposes. In that case, as explained in the next paragraph, registration should not be made until after the work has been published with copyright notice, and should then be applied for on Form A.

PUBLISHED BOOKS OF MUSIC. The correct classification for a published collection of musical compositions depends upon: (a) the nature of the authorship supporting the copyright claim, and (b) the location of the copyright notice on the copies.

○ A published collection containing previously unpublished musical material (including arrangements) should generally be registered as a "musical composition," with an application on Form E, if the copies bear a notice on the title page or first page of music of the collection.
○ A published collection consisting entirely of previously published music, in which the only new matter consists of com-

pilation, text matter, diagrams, or other nonmusical material, should generally be registered as a "book" with an application on Form A. In that case the copies should bear a notice on the title page of the collection or the page immediately following it.

○ An individual composition in a published collection can be registered separately with an application on Form E, if the composition bears its own copyright notice on the title page or first page of music of the composition itself.

COPYRIGHT PROTECTION IN FOREIGN COUNTRIES FOR U.S. MUSICAL COMPOSITIONS

GENERAL INFORMATION. Musical compositions by U.S. citizens can be copyrighted in many foreign countries, but the methods for securing copyright differ. An American author who wishes to secure copyright in a particular country must first determine which of the methods outlined below is appropriate for that country.

Copyright under the Universal Copyright Convention. The United States and about 54 other countries are adherents to the Universal Copyright Convention (the U.C.C.), which came into force on September 16, 1955. Basically, the U.C.C. requires a participating country to give the same protection to foreign works which meet the Convention requirements as it gives to its own domestic works.

The U.C.C. affords protection automatically to unpublished works, without notice, registration, or other formalities. A published musical composition by a U.S. citizen may obtain protection in the other U.C.C. countries, as well as in the United States, if all published copies bear a particular form of copyright notice from the date of their first publication. This notice consists of the symbol ©, accompanied by the name of the copyright owner and the year date of publication. Example:

© John Doe 1968

This notice should be placed on the title page or first page of music. Following publication, the claim to U.S. copyright should be registered in the Copyright Office in the usual way. No registration abroad is necessary to secure copyright.

Copyright under the Buenos Aires Convention. The United States and a number of other Western Hemisphere republics are parties to the Buenos Aires Copyright Convention, signed in 1910. This Convention specifies that authors of any contracting country who have secured copyright in their own country will enjoy in every other contracting country the rights it accords its own works, if the work contains a statement indicating "the reservation of the property right."

Copyright under bilateral arrangements or national laws. The United States has established bilateral copyright relations with a number of foreign countries, some of which are not parties to either the Universal or the Buenos Aires Conventions. In addition, protection for U.S. works may be available in a few other countries under the provisions of their domestic laws. In both cases the extent and requirements of protection will vary from country to country.

Copyright under the Berne Conventions. A large number of countries are members of the International Union for the Protection of Literary and Artistic Works, better known as the Berne Union. Authors of a country that is not a member of the Union, such as the United States, can secure the rights granted by the Berne Conventions, but only if they publish their works first or simultaneously in a country of the Union. What constitutes a bona fide first or simultaneous publication in a particular foreign country may be a difficult legal question.

OTHER INFORMATION ON INTERNATIONAL COPYRIGHT. For further information regarding international copyright matters, request Circular 38 from our Office. We also furnish on request the following current lists showing the copyright relations of various countries:

Circular 38A—International Copyright Relations.
Circular 38B—Berne Union Member Countries.
Circular 38C—Universal Copyright Convention—Accessions Ratifications.

For information about the requirements and protection provided by other countries, it may be advisable to consult an expert familiar with foreign copyright laws. The U.S. Copyright Office is not permitted to recommend agents or attorneys or to give legal advice or information on foreign laws.

Section 1

of

Title 17, U.S. Code

EXCLUSIVE RIGHTS AS TO COPYRIGHTED WORKS.—Any person entitled thereto, upon complying with the provisions of this title, shall have the exclusive right:

(a) To print, reprint, publish, copy, and vend the copyrighted work;

(b) To translate the copyrighted work into other languages or dialects or make any other version thereof, if it be a literary work; to dramatize it if it be a nondramatic work; to convert it into a novel or other nondramatic work if it be a drama; to arrange or adapt it if it be a musical work; to complete, execute, and finish it if it be a model or design for a work of art;

(c) To deliver, authorize the delivery of, read or present the copyrighted work in public for profit if it be a lecture, sermon, address or similar production, or other nondramatic literary work; to make or procure the making of any transcription or record thereof by or from which, in whole or in part, it may in any manner or by any method be exhibited, delivered, presented, produced, or reproduced; and to play or perform it in public for profit, and to exhibit, represent, produce, or reproduce it in any manner or by any method whatsoever. The damages for the infringement by broadcast of any work referred to in this subsection shall not exceed the sum of $100 where the infringing broadcaster shows that he was not aware that he was infringing and that such infringement could not have been reasonably foreseen; and

(d) To perform or represent the copyrighted work publicly if it be a drama or, if it be a dramatic work and not reproduced in copies for sale, to vend any manuscript or any record whatsoever thereof; to make or to procure the making of any transcription or record thereof by or from which, in whole or in part, it may in any manner or by any method be exhibited, performed, represented, produced, or reproduced; and to exhibit, perform, represent, produce, or reproduce it in any manner or by any method whatsoever; and

(e) To perform the copyrighted work publicly for profit if it be a musical composition; and for the purpose of public performance for profit, and for the purposes set forth in subsection (a) hereof, to make any arrangement or setting of it or of the melody of it in any system of notation or any form of record in which the thought of an author may be recorded and from which it may be read or reproduced: *Provided,* That the provisions of this title, so far as they secure copyright controlling the parts of instruments serving to reproduce mechanically the musical work, shall include only compositions published and copyrighted after July 1, 1909, and shall not include the works of a foreign author or composer unless the foreign state or nation of which such author or composer is a citizen or subject grants, either by treaty, convention, agreement, or law, to citizens of the United States similar rights. And as a condition of extending the copyright control to such mechanical reproductions, that whenever the owner of a musical copyright has used or permitted or knowingly acquiesced in the use of the copyrighted work upon the parts of instruments serving to reproduce mechanically the musical work, any other person may make similar use of the copyrighted work upon the payment to the copyright proprietor of a royalty of 2 cents on each such part manufactured, to be paid by the manufacturer thereof; and the copyright proprietor may require, and if so the manufacturer shall furnish, a report under oath on the 20th day of each month on the number of parts of instruments manufactured during the previous month serving to reproduce mechanically said musical work, and royalties shall be due on the parts manufactured during any month upon the 20th of the next succeeding month. The payment of the royalty provided for by this section shall free the articles or devices for which such royalty has been paid from further contribution to the copyright except in case of

159

public performance for profit. It shall be the duty of the copyright owner, if he uses the musical composition himself for the manufacture of parts of instruments serving to reproduce mechanically the musical work, or licenses others to do so, to file notice thereof, accompanied by a recording fee, in the copyright office, and any failure to file such notice shall be a complete defense to any suit, action, or proceeding for any infringement of such copyright.

In case of failure of such manufacturer to pay to the copyright proprietor within thirty days after demand in writing the full sum of royalties due at said rate at the date of such demand, the court may award taxable costs to the plaintiff and a reasonable counsel fee, and the court may, in its discretion, enter judgment therein for any sum in addition over the amount found to be due as royalty in accordance with the terms of this title, not exceeding three times such amount.

The reproduction or rendition of a musical composition by or upon coin-operated machines shall not be deemed a public performance for profit unless a fee is charged for admission to the place where such reproduction or rendition occurs.

(f) To reproduce and distribute to the public by sale or other transfer of ownership, or by rental, lease, or lending, reproductions of the copyrighted work if it be a sound recording: *Provided*, That the exclusive right of the owner of a copyright in a sound recording to reproduce it is limited to the right to duplicate the sound recording in a tangible form that directly or indirectly recaptures the actual sounds fixed in the recording: *Provided further*, That this right does not extend to the making or duplication of another sound recording that is an independent fixation of other sounds, even though such sounds imitate or simulate those in the copyrighted sound recording; or to reproductions made by transmitting organizations exclusively for their own use.

July 1972-8,000

☆ U.S. GOVERNMENT PRINTING OFFICE: 1972-464-237

COPYRIGHT OFFICE

THE LIBRARY OF CONGRESS

WASHINGTON, D.C.   20540

SECTIONS 10, 19, 20

of

Title 17, U. S. Code

SECTION 10. PUBLICATION OF WORK WITH NOTICE.—Any person entitled thereto by this title may secure copyright for his work by publication thereof with the notice of copyright required by this title; and such notice shall be affixed to each copy thereof published or offered for sale in the United States by authority of the copyright proprietor, except in the case of books seeking ad interim protection under section 22 of this title.

SECTION 19. NOTICE; FORM.—The notice of copyright required by section 10 of this title shall consist either of the word "Copyright", the abbreviation "Copr.", or the symbol ©, accompanied by the name of the copyright proprietor, and if the work be a printed literary, musical, or dramatic work, the notice shall include also the year in which the copyright was secured by publication. In the case, however, of copies of works specified in subsections (f) to (k), inclusive, of section 5 of this title, the notice may consist of the letter C enclosed within a circle, thus ©, accompanied by the initials, monogram, mark, or symbol of the copyright proprietor: *Provided,* That on some accessible portion of such copies or of the margin, back, permanent base, or pedestal, or of the substance on which such copies shall be mounted, his name shall appear. But in the case of works in which copyright was subsisting on July 1, 1909, the notice of copyright may be either in one of the forms prescribed herein or may consist of the following words: "Entered according to Act of Congress, in the year   , by A. B., in the office of the Librarian of Congress, at Washington, D. C.," or, at his option, the word "Copyright", together with the year the copyright was entered and the name of the party by whom it was taken out; thus, "Copyright, 19—, by A. B."

SECTION 20. SAME; PLACE OF APPLICATION OF; ONE NOTICE IN EACH VOLUME OR NUMBER OF NEWSPAPER OR PERIODICAL.—The notice of copyright shall be applied, in the case of a book or other printed publication, upon its title page or the page immediately following, or if a periodical either upon the title page, or upon the first page of text of each separate number or under the title heading, or if a musical work either upon its title page or the first page of music. One notice of copyright in each volume or in each number of a newspaper or periodical published shall suffice.

COPYRIGHT OFFICE

THE LIBRARY OF CONGRESS

WASHINGTON, D.C. 20540

SECTION 12

of

Title 17, U.S. Code

WORKS NOT REPRODUCED FOR SALE.—Copyright may also be had of the works of an author, of which copies are not reproduced for sale, by the deposit, with claim of copyright, of one complete copy of such work if it be a lecture or similar production or a dramatic, musical, or dramatico-musical composition; of a title and description, with one print taken from each scene or act, if the work be a motion-picture photoplay; of a photographic print if the work be a photograph; of a title and description, with not less than two prints taken from different sections of a complete motion picture, if the work be a motion picture other than a photoplay; or of a photograph or other identifying reproduction thereof, if it be a work of art or a plastic work or drawing. But the privilege of registration of copyright secured hereunder shall not exempt the copyright proprietor from the deposit of copies, under sections 13 and 14 of this title, where the work is later reproduced in copies for sale.

Application for Registration of a Claim to Copyright in a published book manufactured in the United States of America

Instructions: Make sure that all applicable spaces have been completed before you submit the form. The application must be **SIGNED** at line 10 and the **AFFIDAVIT** (line 11) **must be COMPLETED AND NOTARIZED.** The application should not be submitted until after the date of publication given in line 4, and should state the facts which existed on that date. For further information, see page 4.

Pages 1 and 2 should be typewritten or printed with pen and ink. Pages 3 and 4 should contain exactly the same information as pages 1 and 2, but may be carbon copies. Mail all pages of the application to the Register of Copyrights, Library of Congress, Washington, D.C. 20540, together with 2 copies of the best edition of the work and the registration fee of $6. Make your remittance payable to the Register of Copyrights.

1. Copyright Claimant(s) and Address(es): Give the name(s) and address(es) of the copyright owner(s). Ordinarily the name(s) should be the same as in the notice of copyright on the copies deposited.

Name ....

Address ....

Name ....

Address ....

2. Title: ....

(Give the title of the book as it appears on the title page)

3. Authors: Citizenship and domicile information must be given. Where a work was made for hire, the employer is the author. The citizenship of organizations formed under U.S. Federal or State law should be stated as U.S.A. Authors may be editors, compilers, translators, illustrators, etc., as well as authors of original text. If the copyright claim is based on new matter (see line 5) give requested information about the author of the new matter.

(Give legal name followed by pseudonym if latter appears on the copies)

Domiciled in U.S.A.   Yes ....   No ....   Address ....

Name ....
(Give legal name followed by pseudonym if latter appears on the copies)   Citizenship .... (Name of country)

Domiciled in U.S.A.   Yes ....   No ....   Address ....

Name ....
(Give legal name followed by pseudonym if latter appears on the copies)   Citizenship .... (Name of country)

Domiciled in U.S.A.   Yes ....   No ....   Address ....

4. Date of Publication of This Edition: Give the complete date when copies of this particular edition were first placed on sale, sold, or publicly distributed. The date when copies were made or printed should not be confused with the date of publication. **NOTE:** The full date (month, day, and year) must be given. For further information, see page 4.

....
(Month)   (Day)   (Year)

➤ **(NOTE: Leave line 5 blank unless the following instructions apply to this work.)** ◄

5. New Matter in This Version: If any substantial part of this work has been previously published anywhere, give a brief, general statement of the nature of the new matter published for the first time in this version. New matter may consist of compilation, translation, abridgment, editorial revision, and the like, as well as additional text or pictorial matter.

➤ **NOTE:** | Leave line 6 blank unless there has been a **PREVIOUS FOREIGN EDITION in the English language.** | ◄

6. Book in English Previously Manufactured and Published Abroad: If all or a substantial part of the text of this edition was previously manufactured and published abroad in the English language, complete the following spaces:

Date of first publication of foreign edition ....
(Year)

Was registration for the foreign edition made in the U.S. Copyright Office?   Yes ....   No ....

If your answer is "Yes," give registration number ....

Complete all applicable spaces on next page

EXAMINER

165

7. Deposit account:

8. Send correspondence to:

Name _____ Address _____

9. Send certificate to:

(Type or print name and address)

Name _____

Address _____

(Number and street)

_____

(City)   (State)   (ZIP code)

Information concerning copyright in books

When to Use Form A. Form A is appropriate for published books which have been manufactured in the United States.

What Is a "Book"? The term "books" covers not only material published in book form, but also pamphlets, leaflets, cards, and single pages containing text. Books include fiction, nonfiction, poetry, collections, directories, catalogs, and information in tabular form.

Unpublished Books. The law does not provide for registration of "book" material in unpublished form. Unpublished books are protected at common law against unauthorized use prior to publication.

Duration of Copyright. Statutory copyright in published books lasts for 28 years from the date of first publication, and may be renewed for a second 28-year term.

How to secure statutory copyright in a book

First: Produce Copies With Copyright Notice. Produce the work in copies by printing or other means of reproduction. To secure copyright, it is essential that the copies bear a copyright notice in the required form and position, as explained below.

Second: Publish the Work With Copyright Notice. The copyright law defines the "date of publication" as ". . . the earliest date when copies of the first authorized edition were placed on sale, sold, or publicly distributed by the proprietor of the copyright or under his authority, ..."

Third: Register Your Copyright Claim. Promptly after publica-

Washington, D.C. 20540, two copies of the work as published with notice, an application on Form A, properly completed and notarized, and a fee of $6.

The Copyright Notice. The copyright notice for books shall appear on the title page or verso thereof, and shall consist of three elements: the word "Copyright," or the abbreviation "Copr.," or the symbol ©, accompanied by the name of the copyright owner and the year date of publication. Example: © John Doe 1972. Use of the symbol © may result in securing copyright in countries

Books manufactured abroad

In General. Form A is not appropriate for books which have been manufactured outside the United States.

Foreign-Language Books. Applications covering foreign-language books by foreign authors, manufactured abroad, should be submitted on Form A–B Foreign.

English-Language Books. Books in English manufactured abroad may be registered for "ad interim" copyright (Form A–B Ad Interim); or, if they are protected under the Universal Copyright Convention they are eligible for full-term registration on Form A–B Foreign:

(1) *Ad Interim Copyright.* Ad interim registration is necessary for protection in the United States unless copyright has been secured under the Universal Copyright Convention. To secure ad interim copyright a claim must be registered within 6 months of first publication abroad. Ad interim copyright lasts for 5 years or until an American edition is published within the 5-year period and registered.

(2) *Universal Copyright Convention.* An English-language work by a foreign author first published abroad is eligible for full-term U.S. copyright if: (a) its author is a citizen or subject of a country which is a member of the Universal Copyright Convention, or the work was first published in such country, and (b) all published copies bear the copyright notice provided under the Universal Copyright Convention.

FOR COPYRIGHT OFFICE USE ONLY

Application and affidavit received

Two copies received

Fee received

FORM A–B AD INTERIM

CLASSES	REGISTRATION NO.
A–B	DO NOT WRITE HERE AI AIO BI BIO

Application for Registration of a Claim to Ad Interim Copyright in a book or periodical in the English language manufactured and first published outside the United States of America

Instructions: Make sure that all applicable spaces have been completed before you submit the form. The application must be **SIGNED** at line 9. The application should not be submitted until after the date of publication given in line 4 (a), and should state the facts which existed on that date. For further information, see page 4.

Pages 1 and 2 should be typewritten or printed with pen and ink. Pages 3 and 4 should contain exactly the same information as pages 1 and 2, but may be carbon copies.

Mail all pages of the application to the Register of Copyrights, Library of Congress, Washington, D.C. 20540, U.S.A., together with the material specified in either Option A or B:

Option A: One copy of the work and a fee of $6. Make remittance payable to the Register of Copyrights.

Option B: Two copies of the work and a catalog card. This option is not available if the author was a U. S. citizen or domiciliary on the date of publication, or if the author or proprietor is a citizen, domiciliary, or resident on the date application is filed.

Note: Registration of a claim to ad interim copyright cannot be made under either option unless all of the required items are received in the Copyright Office *within 6 months of the date of first publication.*

1. Copyright Claimant(s) and Address(es): Give the name(s) and address(es) of the copyright owner(s). Ordinarily the name(s) should be the same as in the notice of copyright on the copies deposited. The citizenship of the claimant(s) must be stated.

Name ---

Address --

-------------------- Citizenship -------------------- (Name of country)

Name ---

Address --

-------------------- Citizenship -------------------- (Name of country)

2. Title: *(a)* ---

(Give the title of the work as it appears on the copies)

3. Authors: Citizenship and domicile information must be given. Where a work was made for hire, the employer is the author. Authors may be editors, compilers, translators, illustrators, etc., as well as authors of original text. If the copyright claim is based on new matter (see line 5) give information about the author of the new matter.

Name _____ Citizenship _____
    (Give legal name followed by pseudonym if latter appears on the copies)   (Name of country)

Domiciled in U. S. A. Yes ____ No ____ Address _____

Name _____ Citizenship _____
    (Give legal name followed by pseudonym if latter appears on the copies)   (Name of country)

Domiciled in U. S. A. Yes ____ No ____ Address _____

Name _____ Citizenship _____
    (Give legal name followed by pseudonym if latter appears on the copies)   (Name of country)

Domiciled in U. S. A. Yes ____ No ____ Address _____

4. Publication:

    (a) Date of Publication of This Edition: Give the date when copies of this edition were first placed on sale, sold, or publicly distributed. **NOTE:** The full date (month, day, year) must be given. For further information, see page 4.

    (b) Place of Publication of This Edition: Give the name of the country in which this edition was first published. ◄━

➤ | NOTE: Leave all spaces of line 5 blank unless the instructions below apply to your work. | ◄━

5. New Matter in This Version: If any substantial part of this work has been previously published, give a brief general statement of the nature of the new matter in this version. New matter may consist of compilation, translation, abridgment, editorial revision, and the like, as well as additional text or pictorial matter.

_____

_____

Complete all applicable spaces on next page

EXAMINER

169

6. Deposit account:

7. Send correspondence to:

Name .... Address ....

8. Send certificate to:

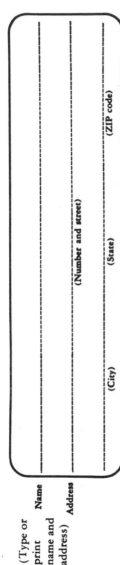

(Type or print name and address)

Name _____

Address _____
(Number and street)

_____
(City)   (State)   (ZIP code)

Information concerning ad interim copyright

Ad Interim Copyright. The law provides that, as a general rule, books and periodicals in the English language must be manufactured in the United States to be protected under United States copyright law. One exception to this requirement is provided in the form of an "ad interim" copyright. Basically, ad interim copyright gives the owner protection for a 5-year term—with the possibility that, if an American edition is manufactured within the 5-year period, the copyright may be extended to the full term.

When to Use Form A–B Ad Interim. Form A–B Ad Interim is appropriate for English-language books and periodicals manufactured and first published outside of the United States—except works which qualify for full term protection under the Universal Copyright Convention, as explained below.

The Universal Copyright Convention (the "U. C. C.")

In General. The Universal Copyright Convention, which came into force on September 16, 1955, provides another exception to the manufacturing requirements, and one which is much broader than ad interim copyright. Any work which qualifies, and which has been published with the copyright notice provided in the Convention, is completely exempted from the manufacturing requirements; full-term (28-year) copyright may be secured without the need of registration in the Copyright Office.

Works Protected Under the U. C. C. A work by a foreign author, first published outside of the United States, is eligible for protection under the Universal Copyright Convention if its author is a citizen of a country which is a party to the Convention, or if the work was first published in such a country.

The U. C. C. Notice. The copyright notice prescribed in the Universal Copyright Convention consists of the symbol ©, accompanied by the name of the copyright proprietor and the year date of first publication. Example: © John Doe 1971. The notice must be located on the work in such a way as to give reasonable notice of the copyright claim.

Registration. Form A–B Ad Interim is not appropriate for works which qualify for protection under the Universal Copyright Convention. If registration for such works is desired, application should be submitted on Form A–B Foreign.

Statutory requirements for ad interim copyright

Time Limits for Ad Interim Registration. In order to secure ad interim copyright, it is essential that registration be made *within six months of the date of first publication outside of the United States.* This means that, without exception, all of the material described in the instructions on page 1 of this form—a properly completed application, copy or copies, and fee or catalog card—must be received in the Copyright Office before the six-month deadline. The date of publication is defined as "... the earliest date when copies of the first authorized edition were placed on sale, sold, or publicly distributed."

The Copyright Notice. No copyright notice is required on the copy or copies of books or periodicals sent to the Copyright Office for ad interim registration. However, the law requires that the notice appear on all other copies brought into the United States. This notice shall consist of the word "Copy-right," the abbreviation "Copr.," or the symbol ©, accompanied by the name of the copyright owner and the year date of publication. For books, the notice shall appear on the title page or verso thereof. For periodicals, the notice shall appear on the title page, the first page of text, or under the title heading.

Importation of Copies. The law permits the importation of 1,500 copies of works for which ad interim registration has been made. The Copyright Office will, in appropriate cases, issue an import statement to be presented to the customs officer at the port of entry.

Extension to Full Copyright Term. The ad interim copyright lasts for 5 years from the date of first publication abroad. The copyright may be extended to the full copyright term if an American edition of the work is manufactured and published during the 5-year period and the claim registered.

FOR COPYRIGHT OFFICE USE ONLY	
Application received	
One copy received	
Two copies received	
Catalog card received	
Fee received	

U.S. GOVERNMENT PRINTING OFFICE:1970—O-410-492

Jan. 1971—25,000

Page 4

171

FORM C

CLASS	REGISTRATION NO.
C	DO NOT WRITE HERE

Application for Registration of a Claim to Copyright in a lecture or similar production prepared for oral delivery

Instructions: Make sure that all applicable spaces have been completed before you submit the form. The application must be **SIGNED** at line 8. For further information, see page 4.

Pages 1 and 2 should be typewritten or printed with pen and ink. Pages 3 and 4 should contain exactly the same information as pages 1 and 2, but may be carbon copies.

Mail all pages of the application to the Register of Copyrights, Library of Congress, Washington, D.C. 20540, together with one complete copy of the work and the registration fee of $6. Make your remittance payable to the Register of Copyrights.

1. Copyright Claimant(s) and Address(es): Give the name(s) and address(es) of the copyright owner(s).

Name ---

Address --

Name ---

Address --

2. Title:

(Give the title of the work as it appears on the copy)

----

3. Authors: Citizenship and domicile information must be given. Where a work is made for hire, the employer is the

Federal or State law should be stated as U.S.A.

If the copyright claim is based on new matter (see line 4)

Name --- Citizenship -------------------
(Give legal name followed by pseudonym if latter appears on the copy)   (Name of country)

Domiciled in U.S.A.   Yes --------   No --------   Address --------------------------------

Name --- Citizenship -------------------
(Give legal name followed by pseudonym if latter appears on the copy)   (Name of country)

Domiciled in U.S.A.   Yes --------   No --------   Address --------------------------------

Name --- Citizenship -------------------
(Give legal name followed by pseudonym if latter appears on the copy)   (Name of country)

Domiciled in U.S.A.   Yes --------   No --------   Address --------------------------------

➡ NOTE: Leave all spaces of line 4 blank unless the instructions below apply to your work. ◀

4. Previous Registration or Publication: If a claim to copy-right in any substantial part of this work was previously registered in the U.S. Copyright Office in unpublished form, or if any substantial part of the work was previously published anywhere, give requested information.

Was work previously registered? Yes ----   No ----   Date of registration ----------   Registration number ----------
Was work previously published?   Yes ----   No ----   Date of publication ----------   Registration number ----------

Is there any substantial **NEW MATTER** in this version? Yes ----   No ------   If your answer is "Yes," give a brief general statement of the nature of the **NEW MATTER** in this version.   (New matter may consist of translation, adaptation, editorial revision, and the like, as well as additional text.)

EXAMINER

Complete all applicable spaces on next page

173

5. Deposit account:

----

6. Send correspondence to:

Name --------------------------------------   Address --------------------------------------

7. Send certificate to:

(Type or print name and address)

Name _____

Address _____

_____

(Number and street)

_____   _____

(City)   (State)   (ZIP code)

Information concerning copyright in works prepared for oral delivery

When to Use Form C. Form C is appropriate for unpublished lectures or similar productions prepared for oral delivery.

What Is a "Work Prepared for Oral Delivery"? This category (Class C) covers the scripts of works prepared *in the first instance* for delivery before an audience, as distinguished from works prepared for publication. Examples include lectures, sermons, addresses, monologs, panel discussions, and variety programs prepared for radio or television. A script submitted for registration in Class C should consist of the actual text of the work to be presented orally.

Unpublished "Books" Not Registrable. The Copyright Office cannot make copyright registration for unpublished "books"—that is, nondramatic literary works which do not qualify for registration in Class C, as explained above.

Unpublished Synopsis. The Copyright Office cannot make registration for unpublished formats, brochures, synopses, or general descriptions of radio and television programs. Likewise, the general idea, outline, or title of a program cannot be copyrighted.

No "Blanket" Copyright. Copyright registration extends only to the material deposited in the Copyright Office. Registration for a script covers the copyrightable material in that script, but does not give any sort of "blanket" protection to future scripts or to a series as a whole.

174

Statutory requirements for copyright in works prepared for oral delivery

How to Register a Claim. To obtain copyright registration, mail to the Register of Copyrights, Library of Congress, Washington, D.C. 20540, one complete copy of the script, an application on Form C, properly completed and signed, and a fee of $6. Manuscripts are not returned, so do not send your only copy.

Procedure to Follow if Work Is Later Published. If the work is later reproduced in copies and published, it is necessary to make a second registration as a "book." Form A is appropriate for books, and the specific requirements for that class are outlined on the form. In general, the law requires that all copies of the published edition contain a copyright notice in the correct form and position. The notice shall appear on the title page or verso thereof, and shall consist of the word "Copyright," the abbreviation "Copr.," or the symbol ©, accompanied by the name of the copyright owner and the year when copyright was secured. Example: © John Doe 1970.

Duration of Copyright. Statutory copyright in unpublished works lasts for 28 years from the date of registration, and may be renewed for a second 28-year term.

FOR COPYRIGHT OFFICE USE ONLY

Application received

One copy received

Fee received

U.S. GOVERNMENT PRINTING OFFICE:1970—O-398-109   Sept. 1970—50,000

Page 4

FORM D

CLASS	REGISTRATION NO.
D	DO NOT WRITE HERE

DF   DFO   DP   DU

Application for Registration of a Claim to Copyright
in a dramatic or dramatico-musical composition

Instructions: Make sure that all applicable spaces have been completed before you submit the form. The application must be **SIGNED** at line 9. For published works the application should not be submitted until after the date of publication given in line 4 (*a*), and should state the facts which existed on that date. For further information, see page 4.

Pages 1 and 2 should be typewritten or printed with pen and ink. Pages 3 and 4 should contain exactly the same information as pages 1 and 2, but may be carbon copies.

Mail all pages of the application to the Register of Copyrights, Library of Congress, Washington, D.C. 20540, together with:

(*a*) If unpublished, one complete copy of the work and the registration fee of $6.

(*b*) If published, two copies of the best edition of the work and the registration fee of $6.

Make your remittance payable to the Register of Copyrights.

1. Copyright Claimant(s) and Address(es): Give the name(s) and address(es) of the copyright owner(s). In the case of published works the name(s) should ordinarily be the same as in the notice of copyright on the copies deposited.

Name --

Address ---

Name --

Address ---

2. Title: ---

(Give the title of the dramatic or dramatico-musical composition as it appears on the copies)

3. Authors: Citizenship and domicile information must be given. Where a work is made for hire, the employer is the author. The citizenship of organizations formed under U.S. Federal or State

Authors may be editors, translators, etc., as well as authors of original dramatic material. If the copyright claim is based on new matter (see line 5) give information about the author of the new

(Give legal name followed by pseudonym if latter appears on the copies)

(Name of country)

Domiciled in U.S.A. Yes _____ No _____ Address _____

Name _____
(Give legal name followed by pseudonym if latter appears on the copies)

Citizenship _____
(Name of country)

Domiciled in U.S.A. Yes _____ No _____ Address _____

Name _____
(Give legal name followed by pseudonym if latter appears on the copies)

Citizenship _____
(Name of country)

Domiciled in U.S.A. Yes _____ No _____ Address _____

➡ NOTE: | Leave all spaces of line 4 blank unless your work has been PUBLISHED. | ◀

4. (a) Date of Publication: Give the date when copies of this particular version of the work were first placed on sale, sold, or publicly distributed. The date when copies were made or printed, or the date when the work was performed should not be confused with the date of publication. NOTE: The full date (month, day, and year) must be given.

_____   _____   _____
(Month)   (Day)   (Year)

(b) Place of Publication: Give the name of the country in which this particular version of the work was first published.

➡ NOTE: | Leave all spaces of line 5 blank unless the instructions below apply to your work. | ◀

5. Previous Registration or Publication: If a claim to copyright in any substantial part of this work was previously registered in the U.S. Copyright Office in unpublished form, or if a substantial part of the work was previously published anywhere, give requested information.

Was work previously registered? Yes _____ No _____ Date of registration _____ Registration number _____

Was work previously published? Yes _____ No _____ Date of publication _____ Registration number _____

Is there any substantial **NEW MATTER** in this version? Yes _____ No _____   If your answer is "Yes," give a brief general statement of the nature of the **NEW MATTER** in this version. (New matter may consist of translation, dramatization, editorial revision, and the like, as well as additional text or musical material.)

_____

Complete all applicable spaces on next page

EXAMINER

177

6. Deposit account:

7. Send correspondence to:

Name _____ Address _____

8. Send certificate to:

(Type or
Print
name and
address

Name _____

Address _____

(Number and street)

_____
(City)

_____
(State)

_____
(ZIP Code)

Information concerning copyright in dramatic or dramatico-musical compositions

When to Use Form D. Form D is appropriate for unpublished and published dramatic compositions and dramatico-musical compositions.

What Is a "Dramatic Composition" or "Dramatico-Musical Composition"? This category (Class D) covers the acting versions of dramatic works such as plays, radio or television dramas, musical comedies, motion picture shooting scripts, operas, choreographic works of a dramatic character, pantomimes, and the like. For registration in Class D a work must be more than a story or synopsis that is potentially capable of being dramatized. It should tell its story by means of dialogue and dramatic action rather than through narrative or descriptive material, and it should be complete enough for dramatic performance in its present form.

Unpublished "Books" Not Registrable. Stories, scenarios, and narrative outlines are considered "books," and cannot be registered for copyright in unpublished form.

No "Blanket" Copyright. The general idea, outline, or title for a play or dramatic series cannot be copyrighted. Registration for a script covers the copyrightable material in that script, but does not give any sort of "blanket" protection to future scripts or to a series as a whole.

Duration of Copyright. Statutory copyright begins on the date the work was first published, or if the work was registered for copyright in unpublished form, copyright begins on the date of registration. In either case copyright lasts for 28 years, and may be renewed for a second 28-year term.

Unpublished dramatic compositions

How to Register a Claim. To obtain copyright registration, mail to the Register of Copyrights, Library of Congress, Washington, D.C. 20540, one complete copy of the dramatic work, an application on Form D, properly completed and signed, and a fee

Procedure to Follow if Work Is Later Published. If the work is later reproduced in copies and published, it is necessary to make a second registration, following the procedure outlined below. To maintain copyright protection, all copies of the published edition must contain a copyright notice in the required form and

Published dramatic compositions

What Is "Publication"? Publication, generally, means the sale, placing on sale, or public distribution of copies. Dramatic performance is not generally regarded as "publication."

How to Secure Copyright in a Published Dramatic Composition:

1. Produce copies with copyright notice, by printing or other means of reproduction.
2. Publish the work.
3. Register the copyright claim, following the instructions on page 1 of this form.

The Copyright Notice. In order to secure and maintain copyright protection in a published work, it is essential that all copies published in the United States contain the statutory copyright notice. This notice shall appear on the title page or verso thereof, and shall consist of three elements:

1. *The word "Copyright," the abbreviation "Copr.," or the symbol* ©. Use of the symbol © may result in securing copyright in countries which are members of the Universal Copyright Convention.

2. *The year date of publication.* This is ordinarily the date when copies were first placed on sale, sold, or publicly distributed. However, if the work has been registered for copyright in unpublished form, the notice should contain the year of registration; or, if there is new copyrightable matter in the published edition, it is advisable to include both dates.

3. *The name of the copyright owner (or owners).*

Example: © John Doe 1970.

NOTE: If copies are published without the required notice, the right to secure copyright is lost and cannot be restored.

FOR COPYRIGHT OFFICE USE ONLY

Application received	
One copy received	
Two copies received	
Fee received	

Application

for Registration of a Claim to Copyright

In a musical composition the author of which is a citizen or domiciliary of the United States of America or which was first published in the United States of America

Instructions: Make sure that all applicable spaces have been completed before you submit the form. The application must be **SIGNED** at line 9. For published works the application should not be submitted until after the date of publication given in line 4(a), and should state the facts which existed on that date. For further information, see page 4.

Pages 1 and 2 should be typewritten or printed with pen and ink. Pages 3 and 4 should contain exactly the same information as pages 1 and 2, but may be carbon copies.

1. Copyright Claimant(s) and Address(es): Give the name(s) and address(es) of the copyright owner(s). In the case of published works the name(s) should ordinarily be the same as in the notice of copyright on the copies deposited.

Mail all pages of the application to the Register of Copyrights, Library of Congress, Washington, D.C. 20540, together with:

    (a) If unpublished, one complete copy of the work and the registration fee of $6.

    (b) If published, two copies of the best edition of the work and the registration fee of $6.

Make your remittance payable to the Register of Copyrights.

FORM E

REGISTRATION NO.	CLASS
DO NOT WRITE HERE EP EU	**E**

Name --

Address --

Name --

Address --

2. Title: --

(Give the title of the musical composition as it appears on the copies)

3. Authors: Citizenship and domicile information must be given. Where a work is made for hire, the employer is the author. Organizations formed under U.S. Federal or State

Authors include composers of music, authors of words, arrangers, compilers, etc. If the copyright claim is based on new matter (see line 5) give information about the author of the

Domiciled in U.S.A. Yes ---- No ---- Address ----------------------------------- Author of ------------------------- Other ----------------------
(Give legal name followed by pseudonym if latter appears on the copies) Citizenship: U.S.A. ------- (Name of country)
(Check if U.S. citizen) (State which: words, music, arrangement, etc.)

Name ---
(Give legal name followed by pseudonym if latter appears on the copies)

Domiciled in U.S.A. Yes ---- No ---- Address ----------------------------------- Author of ------------------------- Other ----------------------
Citizenship: U.S.A. ------- (Name of country)
(Check if U.S. citizen) (State which: words, music, arrangement, etc.)

Name ---
(Give legal name followed by pseudonym if latter appears on the copies)

Domiciled in U.S.A. Yes ---- No ---- Address ----------------------------------- Author of ------------------------- Other ----------------------
Citizenship: U.S.A. ------- (Name of country)
(Check if U.S. citizen) (State which: words, music, arrangement, etc.)

➡ NOTE: Leave all spaces of line 4 blank unless your work has been PUBLISHED. ◄

4. (a) Date of Publication: Give the date when copies of this particular version of the work were first placed on sale, sold, or publicly distributed. The date when copies were made

or printed, or the date when the work was performed should not be confused with the date of publication. NOTE: The full date (month, day, and year) must be given.

----------------------------------- ----------------------------------- -----------------------------------
(Month) (Day) (Year)

(b) Place of Publication: Give the name of the country in which this particular version of the work was first published.

➡ NOTE: Leave all spaces of line 5 blank unless the instructions below apply to your work. ◄

5. Previous Registration or Publication: If a claim to copyright in any substantial part of this work was previously registered in the U.S. Copyright Office in unpublished form,

or if any substantial part of the work was previously published anywhere, give requested information.

Was work previously registered? Yes ---- No ---- Date of registration ----------------- Registration number ----------------

Was work previously published? Yes ---- No ---- Date of publication ----------------- Registration number ----------------

Is there any substantial **NEW MATTER** in this version? Yes ------- No ------- If your answer is "Yes," give a brief general statement of the nature of the **NEW MATTER** in this version. (New matter may consist of compilation, arrangement, adaptation, editorial revision, and the like, as well as additional words and music.)

Complete all applicable spaces on next page

EXAMINER

181

Information concerning copyright in musical compositions

When to Use Form E. Form E is appropriate for unpublished and published musical compositions by authors who are U.S. citizens or domiciliaries, and for musical compositions first published in the United States.

What Is a "Musical Composition"? The term "musical composition" includes compositions consisting of music alone, or of words and music combined. It also includes arrangements and other versions of earlier compositions, if new copyrightable work of authorship has been added.

—*Song Lyrics Alone.* The term "musical composition" does not include song poems and other works consisting of words without music. Works of that type are not registrable for copyright in unpublished form.

—*Sound Recordings.* Phonograph records, tape recordings, and other sound recordings are not regarded as "copies" of the musical compositions recorded on them, and are not acceptable for copyright registration. For purposes of deposit, the musical compositions should be written in some form of legible notation. If the composition contains words, they should be written above or beneath the notes to which they are sung.

Duration of Copyright. Statutory copyright begins on the date the work was first published, or, if the work was registered for copyright in unpublished form, copyright begins on the date of registration. In either case, copyright lasts for 28 years, and may be renewed for a second 28-year term.

Unpublished musical compositions

How to Register a Claim. To obtain copyright registration, mail to the Register of Copyrights, Library of Congress, Washington, D.C. 20540, one complete copy of the musical composition, an application Form E, properly completed and

Procedure to Follow if Work Is Later Published. If the work is later reproduced in copies and published, it is necessary to make a second registration, following the procedure outlined below. To maintain copyright protection, all copies

Published musical compositions

What Is "Publication"? Publication, generally, means the sale, placing on sale, or public distribution of copies. Limited distribution of so-called "professional" copies ordinarily would not constitute publication. However, since the dividing line between a preliminary distribution and actual publication may be difficult to determine, it is wise for the author to affix notice of copyright to copies that are to be circulated beyond his control.

How to Secure Copyright in a Published Musical Composition:

1. *Produce copies with copyright notice,* by printing or other means of reproduction.
2. *Publish the work.*
3. *Register the copyright claim,* following the instructions on page 1 of this form.

The Copyright Notice. In order to secure and maintain copyright protection for a published work, it is essential that all copies published in the United States contain the statutory copyright notice. This notice shall appear on the title page or first page of music and must consist of three elements:

1. *The word "Copyright," the abbreviation "Copr.," or the symbol* ©. Use of the symbol © may result in securing copyright in countries which are parties to the Universal Copyright Convention.
2. *The year date of publication.* This is ordinarily the date when copies were first placed on sale, sold, or publicly distributed. However, if the work has been registered for copyright in unpublished form, the notice should contain the year of registration; or, if there is new copyrightable matter in the published version, it should include both dates.
3. *The name of the copyright owner (or owners).* Example:

© John Doe **1972.**

NOTE: If copies are published without the required notice the right to secure copyright is lost and cannot be restored.

U.S. GOVERNMENT PRINTING OFFICE :1972—O-454-207

Feb. 1972—500,000

Page 4

183

FORM R

REGISTRATION NO.
DO NOT WRITE HERE

Application for Registration of a Claim to Renewal Copyright

Instructions: Make sure that all applicable spaces have been completed before you submit the form. The application must be **SIGNED** at line 8. For further information, see page 4.

Pages 1 and 2 should be typewritten or printed with pen and ink. Pages 3 and 4 should contain exactly the same information as pages 1 and 2, but may be carbon copies.

Mail all pages of the application to the Register of Copyrights, Library of Congress, Washington, D.C. 20540, together with the registration fee of $4. Make your remittance payable to the Register of Copyrights.

1. Renewal Claimant(s), Address(es), and Statement of Claim: Give the full name(s) and mailing address(es) of the claimant(s) of the renewal copyright. State the statutory category of each renewal claimant. It must be one of the categories described on Page 4.

(*a*) Name --

Address --

Claiming as --
(Use the appropriate statement appearing on page 4)

(*b*) Name --

Address --

Claiming as --
(Use the appropriate statement appearing on page 4)

(*c*) Name --

Address --

2. (a) Title: Give the full title of the work. In the case of music, give specific instrumentation.

....

....

(b) Renewable Matter: If the work was a new version of a previous work, renewal may be claimed only in the new matter. If this work was a new version, state in general the new matter (e.g., arrangement, editing, illustrations, translations, etc.) upon which copyright was claimed.

....

(c) Contribution to Periodical or Other Composite Work: If the work was a contribution, give the title of the periodical or composite work in which it was published. ....

If a periodical, give: Vol. ....; No. ....; Issue Date ....

3. Authors of Renewable Matter: Give the names of all authors who contributed copyrightable matter to this version, but not the names of authors of previous versions. ....

....

4. Facts of Original Registration: The facts given here must agree with the Copyright Office records of the original registration.

Original registration number: Class ....; No. ....

If registered as published, give date of publication ....

$\qquad\qquad$ (Month) $\qquad$ (Day) $\qquad$ (Year)

If registered as unpublished, give date of registration ....

$\qquad\qquad$ (Month) $\qquad$ (Day) $\qquad$ (Year)

Original copyright claimant ....

$\qquad$ (Name of claimant in original registration) $\qquad$ **Complete all applicable spaces on next page**

EXAMINER

185

5. Deposit account:

....

6. Send correspondence to:

Name ....   Address ....

7. Send certificate to:

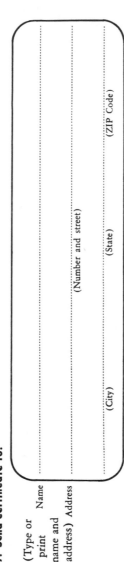

(Type or
print   Name ....
name and
address) Address ....
                    (Number and street)

....
(City)   (State)   (ZIP Code)

Information concerning renewal copyright

Two important points must be kept in mind with respect to renewal copyright: (1) there are strict time limits for securing it, and (2) it can be claimed only by certain specified persons named in the law.

Time limits

When to renew. The original term of copyright in a published work lasts for 28 years from the date of publication; in the case of a work originally registered in unpublished form, the copyright term lasts for 28 years from the date of registration in the Copyright Office. In either case, the copyright may be renewed for a second 28-year term only if a claim is registered in the Copyright Office within the last (28th) year of the original copyright term. For example, a work copyrighted on June 15, 1943, would be eligible for renewal between June 15, 1970, and June 15, 1971.

Caution: Unless a valid renewal claim and fee are *received* in the Copyright Office before the first copyright term expires, copyright protection is lost permanently and the work enters the public domain. The Copyright Office has no discretion to extend the renewal time limits.

How to register your claim

Procedure to follow. Complete an application for renewal registration on Form R and send it to the Register of Copyrights, Washington, D.C. 20540. The application should be accompanied by the registration fee of $4. Do not send copies of the work.

Except in the case of four specific types of works, the law gives the right to claim renewal to the individual author of the work, regardless of who owned the copyright during the original term. If the author is deceased, the statute gives the right to claim renewal to certain of his statutory beneficiaries as explained below. The present owner (proprietor) of a copyright is entitled to claim renewal *only* in the cases listed in Paragraph B, below.

A. The following persons may claim renewal in all types of works except those enumerated in Paragraph B, below:

  1. The author, if living. State the claim as: *the author.*

  2. The widow, widower, and/or children of the author, if the author is not living. State the claim as: *the widow (widower) of the author* ------------ and/or *the child*
                                (Name of author)
    (*children*) *of the deceased author* ------------
                                 (Name of author)

  3. The author's executor(s), if the author left a will and

    if there is no surviving widow, widower, or child. State the claim as: *the executor(s) of the author* ------------
                                   (Name of author)

  4. The next of kin of the author, if the author left no will and if there is no surviving widow, widower, or child. State the claim as: *the next of kin of the deceased author*
    ------------ *there being no will.*
    (Name of author)

B. In the case of the following four types of works, the proprietor (owner of the copyright at the time of renewal registration) may claim renewal:

  1. Posthumous work (work first published and copyrighted after the death of the author). State the claim as: *proprietor of copyright in a posthumous work.*

  2. Periodical, cyclopedic, or other composite work. State the claim as: *proprietor of copyright in a composite work.*

  3. "Work copyrighted by a corporate body otherwise than as assignee or licensee of the individual author." State the

claim as: *proprietor of copyright in a work copyrighted by a corporate body otherwise than as assignee or licensee of the individual author.* (This type of claim is considered appropriate in relatively few cases.)

  4. Work copyrighted by an employer for whom such work was made for hire. State the claim as: *proprietor of copyright in a work made for hire.*

FOR COPYRIGHT OFFICE USE ONLY

Application received

Fee received

GPO : 1970 O - 409-555

Jan. 1971—75,000

Page 4

187

CHAPTER 22

THE MOTION PICTURE AS
BUNDLE OF RIGHTS

"PROPERTY. That which is peculiar or proper to any person; that which belongs exclusively to one; in the strict legal sense, an aggregate of rights which are guaranteed and protected by the government. Fulton Light, Heat & Power Co. v. State, 65 Misc. Rep. 263, 121 N.Y.S. 536."

This definition is one of many definitions of PROPERTY given in BLACK'S LAW DICTIONARY (4th ed, 1951).

The motion picture production company collects a lot of rights from a lot of people.

1. COPYRIGHT

An author of a book has a copyright in his book (let's call it "THE MYSTERY OF THE LOVING BABY EATERS WEST OF MARS" to give the picture a romantic-horror-western-science fiction flavor).

The motion picture production company may seek to obtain not just "the rights to make a motion picture based on the book." but also: "(i) all motion picture rights, including silent, sound, dialogue, talking, musical, television, motion picture and dramatic rights (except live stage rights) and all distribution and exhibition rights, (ii) the right to adapt, change and modify the work, (iii) the right to translate the motion picture version of the work into any and all languages, (iv) the right to advertise and exploit the motion picture in all media, including the right to synopsize the motion picture version, (vi) remake, reissue and sequel rights, (vii) recording rights and the right to make commercial phonograph records and tapes, (viii) live television rights, the right of first refusal for such rights, or a restriction on the exercise by the author for a given number of years of live television rights reserved by him, (ix) novelization rights to an original screenplay and to motion picture sequels, (x) the right to use the title of the basic work, (xi) the copyright of the motion picture and the right to secure copyright and renewal of same, (xii) character rights for commercial tieups and for merchandising, (xiii) television series rights and character rights for television series and sequels, and (xiv) subscription television rights, (xv) additional rights."

SUBSIDIARY RIGHTS AND RESIDUALS edited by Joseph Taubman, page 33, Chapter 5 "Subsidiary Rights And Residuals In Motion Pictures" by Harold S. Klein.

Even after the author of the book "THE MYSTERY OF THE LOVING BABY EATERS WEST OF MARS" has given the above rights to the motion picture company, the author retains many rights (including, but not limited to, the copyright in the book, the right to use the characters in additional books, etc.).

2. RIGHTS IN FICTITIOUS CHARACTERS

"The instruments under which Warner claims were prepared by Warner Bros. Corporation which is a large, experienced moving picture producer. It would seem proper, therefore, to construe the instruments under the assumption that the claimant knew what it wanted and that in defining the items in the instruments which it desired and intended to take, it included all of the items it was contracting to take. We are of the opinion that since the use of characters and character names are nowhere specifically mentioned in the agreements, but that other items, including the title, "The Maltese Falcon," and their use are specifically mentioned as being granted, that the character rights with the names cannot be held to be within the grants, and that under the doctrine of *ejusdem generis*, general language cannot be held to include them. As was said in Phillip v. Jerome H. Remick & Co., S.D., N.Y., Op. No. 9,999, 1936, 'Such doubt as there is should be resolved in favor of the composer. The clearest language is necessary to divest the author of the fruits of his labor. Such language is lacking here.' See, also, Tobani v. Carl Fischer, Inc., 1942, 263 App.Div. 503, 507, 33 N.Y.S.2d 294, 299, affirmed 1942, 289 N.Y. 727, 46 N.E.2d 347.

The conclusion that these rights are not within the granting instruments is strongly buttressed by the fact that historically and presently detective fiction writers have and do carry the leading characters with their names and individualisms from one story into succeeding stories. This was the practice of Edgar Allen Poe, Sir Arthur Conan Doyle, and others; and in the last two decades of S. S. Van Dine, Earle Stanley Gardner, and others. The reader's interest thereby snowballs as new "capers" of the familiar characters are related in succeeding tales. If the intention of the contracting parties had been to avoid this practice which was a very valuable one to the author, it is hardly reasonable that it would be left to a general clause following specific grants. Another buttressing fact is that Hammett wrote and caused to be published in 1932, long after the Falcon agreements, three stories in which some of the leading characters of the Falcon were featured, and no objection was voiced by Warner. It is also of some note that the evidence shows that Columbia, long subsequent to the conveying instruments, dickered with Warner for the use of the Falcon on its "Suspense" radio program and, failing in its efforts, substituted "The Kandy Tooth" which uses the Falcon characters under license of Hammett. Warner made no claim against Columbia at or reasonably soon afterward. The conclusion we have come to, as to the intention of the parties, would seem to be in harmony with the fact that the purchase price paid by Warner was $8,500.00, which would seem inadequate compensation for the complete surrender of the characters made famous by the popular reception of the book, The Maltese Falcon; and that the intention of the parties, inclusive of the 'Assignment,' was not that Hammett should be deprived of using the Falcon characters in subsequently written stories, and that the contract, properly construed, does not deprive Hammett of their use."

WARNER BROS. PICTURES V. COLUMBIA BROADCASTING SYSTEM, DASHIELL HAMMETT, etc. (1954). 216 Fed. Rep. 2d 945, 949-950.

3. RIGHTS TO USE ACTORS' FACES, ETC.

The right of privacy, the right of publicity, the right to commercially exploit one's name, likeness, performance will be called "right of privacy" in this discussion.

An actor has rights of privacy. There have been some legal decisions that these rights are *personal* rights (and thus die when the author dies), and there have been some legal decisions that one or more of these rights of privacy are *property* rights (and thus survive the death of the actor and become part of his estate).

The following is an extract of a 1948 contract between Roy Rogers and Republic Pictures Corporation.

"The 1948 contract, paragraph 4: '(A) The Artist hereby

190

grants to Producer the sole and exclusive right to his services for motion picture purposes during the term hereof * * * to photograph and/or otherwise reproduce any and all of his acts, poses, plays and appearances * * * and to record his voice and all instrumental, musical and other sound effects produced by him * * * The Artist also grants to the Producer, solely and exclusively, all rights of every kind and character whatsoever in and to all such photographs, reproductions and recordings and all other results and proceeds of his services hereunder, perpetually, and also the perpetual right to use the Artist's name and pictures or other reproductions of his physical likeness and recordations and reproductions of his voice, in connection with the advertising and exploitation thereof * * *.

'(B) For the purpose of advertising the photoplays to be produced hereunder, and subject to the reservations set forth in Sub-paragraph (C) of this Paragraph 4, the Artist also hereby grants to the Producer the right, during the term hereof, to use and/or authorize the use of his name and/or likeness in so-called 'commercial advertising,' to wit, advertising relating to products other than motion pictures, (subject to a number of limitations.)

'(C) The Artist reserves to himself the right to enter into any and all commercial tie-ups for products of every kind or character (other than motion pictures) * * *.' "

REPUBLIC PICTURES CORP. ET AL. V. ROY ROGERS. (9th Circuit, 1954) 213 F.2d 662. 101 USPQ475. 29 C.O. Bull. 342, 44-45.

The following is an extract of a 1946 contract between Gene Autry and Republic Pictures Inc.

"The producer shall have the right to photograph and/or otherwise reproduce any and all of the *acts, poses, plays and appearances* of the artist of any and all kinds during each employment period, and to record for motion picture purposes the voice of the artist and all instrumental, musical and other sound effects produced by him hereunder, and to reproduce and/or transmit the same in connection with such *acts, poses, plays and appearances* as the producer may desire, and the producer shall own solely and exclusively all rights of every kind and character whatsoever in and to the same perpetually, including the right to use and exploit all or any part of the same in such manner as the producer may desire, and including, as well, the perpetual right to use the name and likeness of the artist and recordations and reproductions of his voice in connection with the advertising and exploitation thereof. The artist does hereby also grant to the producer the right to make use of and to allow others to make use of his name (in addition to and other than in connection with the *acts, poses, plays and appearances* of the artist hereunder), for the purpose of *advertising, exploiting and/or publicizing photoplays* in which the artist appears, as well as the right to make use of and distribute and to allow others to make use of and distribute his pictures, photographs and other reproductions of his physical likeness and of his voice for the like purpsoe. The producer shall also have the right to 'double' or 'dub' the *acts, poses, plays and appearances* of the artist hereunder and, as well, his voice and/or sound effects produced by him hereunder to such extent as the producer may desire. The rights granted to the producer in this paragraph shall inure not only to the benefit of the producer, but also the benefit of all persons who may hereafter acquire from the producer the right to distribute, transmit, exhibit, advertise and/or exploit the photoplays in which the artist appears hereunder." (Emphasis supplied.)

AUTRY V. REPUBLIC PICTURES, INC. (U.S. District Court, Southern District, California, 1954) 104 F. Supp. 918. 93USPQ284. 28 C.O. Bull. 20, 23.

The following is an extract from a 1930 contract between Bela Lugosi and Universal Pictures Company, Inc.

"The producer shall have the right to photograph and/or otherwise produce, reproduce, transmit, exhibit, distribute, and exploit in connection with the said photoplay any and all of the artist's acts, poses, plays and appearances of any and all kinds hereunder, and shall further have the right to record, reproduce, transmit, exhibit, distribute, and exploit in connection with said photoplay the artist's voice, and all instrumental, musical, and other sound effects produced by the artist in connection with such acts, poses, plays and appearances. The producer shall likewise have the right to use and give publicity to the artist's name and likeness, photographic or otherwise, and to recordations and reproductions of the artist's voice and all instrumental, musical, and other sound effects produced by the artist hereunder, in connection with the advertising and exploitation of said photoplay."

BELA GEORGE LUGOSI V. UNIVERSAL PICTURES COMPANY (1972). (Superior Court, California, Los Angeles No. 877 975) 3 PERFORMING ARTS REVIEW, 19, 21-22.

4. COLLECTING RIGHTS

A motion picture production company may utilize the services of the writer of the original book to also write the screenplay. *Or* there may be two writers from whom the motion picture production company has to collect rights. (1) The book writer. (2) The screenplay writer.

An episode in a motion picture series or television series may be written by a writer other than the writers who created the continuing characters. The production company has to collect rights to use the characters.

Each actor, whether or not he has a detailed written contract with the production company, expressly and/or impliedly gives up certain right of privacy rights to the company.

The motion picture may use a title which may or may not be connected to any copyright use in the movie. The value may lie in the title having been that of a successful song or book. The motion picture production company must collect the rights to use the title.

The motion picture production company must collect copyright rights in the music, rights in the recording of the soundtrack used in the picture.

The motion picture production company must collect the rights from the many persons who are given credits to use their names on film credits, in publicity and advertising and to authorize others to so use these names.

The above illustrations of rights collected by motion picture production companies is not intended to be a listing of all rights.

More rights will be mentioned in the next chapter dealing with UNAUTHORIZED USERS.

CHAPTER 23

UNAUTHORIZED USERS

Pirates

In the early days, around 1900, films were not rented, but prints were sold outright by the foot.

During these days some pornographic pictures are not rented out to exhibitors, but prints are sold outright for a flat fee.

In the early days of motion pictures, people made unauthorized copies of prints.

This is still done. According to a TV Guide article, (October 28, 1972, issue, pages 11-14), the Federal Bureau of Investigation is involved in fighting film pirates.

Numerous motion pictures are in the public domain *as far as copyright law is concerned*. Possibly the common law copyright expired and the picture was not covered by statutory copyright. Possibly the original statutory period of 28 years expired, and no Renewal period copyright was obtained.

Therefore, if a U.S. copier (pirate) of such a public domain film is sued in the U.S. on a copyright infringement theory, then the copier could win.

But, what would happen if such a pirate is sued on other theories?

What would happen, if an actor sued the pirate for *invasion of rights of privacy*? The actor would allege in a complaint that he owns his right of privacy, that he has authorized the film production company (and its authorized distributors and exhibitors), and that he has not authorized the pirate to use the actor's name, face, likeness, *acts, poses, plays and appearances*. Could the actor then enjoin the duplication and exhibition of the motion picture because the actor's right

194

of privacy has been infringed upon?

If a fictitious character has an existence separate from the stories about him, on a theory other than copyright, then would the owner of a character used in a public domain movie be able to successfully sue a pirate for unauthorizedly using the fictitious character?

Sears and Compco

The *Sears* and *Compco* cases are often cited for the quotes which follow.

"But because of the federal patent laws a State may not, when the article is unpatented and uncopyrighted, prohibit the copying of the article itself or award damages for such copying. Cf. G. Ricordi & Co. v. Haendler, 194 F2d 914, 916 (CA2d Cir 1952). The judgment below did both and in so doing gave Stiffel the equivalent of a patent monopoly on its unpatented lamp. That was error, and Sears is entitled to a judgment in its favor." SEARS ROEBUCK & CO. v. STIFFEL 376US225, 232-233. 84SC + 784. II LEd2d 661, 667-8. (1964).

". . . when an article is unprotected by a patent or copyright, state law may not forbid others to copy that article. To forbid copying would interfere with the federal policy, found in Article I, Section 8, Clause 8 of the Constitution and in the implementing federal statutes, of allowing free access to copy whatever the federal patent and copyright laws leave in the public domain." COMPCO. CORP. v. DAY-BRITE LIGHTING, INC. 376 US 234, 237. 84 SCT.779.11LEd2d 669, 672. (1964).

Ricordi

In the Ricordi case, defendant *copied* a book by the *method of photocopying* it. Please remember that there are other ways of *copying* a book then by the *method of photocopying*.

"The plaintiff concedes — as we infer and as in any event it would be obliged to do — that upon the expiration of the copyright the defendant was free to copy the libretto and the scores word for word and note for note; but it asserts that he was not free to do so by photographing the pages of its copyrighted book as he did, because the typography was the plaintiff's creation and became in some sense its "property." This typography, it says, being the work of its skilled engravers, was more than the product of ordinary manual craftsmanship, but it was not dedicated to the public when the copyright was taken out on the book . . .

". . . if the especial typography was itself copyrightable, it too was dedicated to the public (after the copyright in the libretto and scores expired), for it was certainly part of the "work." Therefore we need consider only the possibility that the typography was not copyrightable. . . . the "work," appearing as it did with an unlimited copyright notice, would give notice to the public of a claim to the protection of the Copyright Act over all that appeared in it; and that would imply that, when the copyright expired, the "work" in all its aspects would be in the public demesne. After the copyright did expire the public would certainly understand that they might reproduce the book without any limitation, and if it was permissible to prevent their doing so photographically, that expectation would be defeated . . .

"For the foregoing reasons we hold that the defendant was free to photgraph and sell the plaintiff's book . . ." G. RICORDI & CO. v. HAENDLER (1952) 194 F2d 914. 92USPQ340. 28 C.O. Bull. 419, 421, 422.

It was this Ricordi case which the Supreme Court cited after writing "a State may not, when the article is unpatented and uncopyrighted, prohibit the copying of the article itself or award damages for such copying."

Grove Press v. Collectors Publications

In the Grove v. Collectors case, defendant *copied* a book by the *method of photocopying* it. Please remember that there are other ways of copying a book than by the *method of photocopying*.

"The words in an uncopyrightable book are in the public domain and may be copied by anyone without infringing any copyright. Such copying, alone, does not constitute unfair competition. *Sears . . . Compco . . .*

"Unfair appropriation of the property of a competitor is unfair competition and redressable in a situation of this kind in spite of the holdings in *Sears . . . Compco . . .*

". . . In view of Plaintiff's expenditure of substantial sums

196

in setting type and in engraving plates, it would constitute unfair competition for Defendants to appropriate the value and benefit of such expenditure to themselves by photographing and reproducing Plaintiff's book through the offset-lithography process, thereby cutting their own costs and obtaining an unfair competetive advantage.'' GROVE PRESS, INC. v. COLLECTORS PUBLICATIONS, INC. (1967) (U.S. District Court, Central District, California). 264 F.Supp. 603, 606-7. 152 USPQ 787. 36 C.D. Bull. 286, 291.

Commentary

Just because some law is established, even at Supreme Court level, does not guarantee that a trial court judge will follow that law in the case in front of him. The trial court may consider that the law is not applicable to the facts at hand.

A court may have in front of it a case in which defendant *copied* by the method of *photocopying* the visual portions of a motion picture. Will the trial court apply the Ricordi case, which was cited by the Supreme Court; or will the trial court apply the Grove v. Collectors case? The lawyer for the defendant will want the Ricordi law to be applied. The lawyer for the plaintiff will want the Grove v. Collectors law to be applied.

On which side will your bread and butter lie? Will you be the plaintiff or the pirate?

CHAPTER 24

MOTION PICTURE MUSIC

There are various possible contracts between a Producer and a Composer. Such contracts may cover points including:

1. Producer hereby employs and engages Composer to render his services for and during the period of this Agreement to write and compose such songs and other musical compositions for the motion picture tentatively entitled . . .

2. Composer hereby accepts such employment . . .

3. The term of this Agreement . . .

4. Producer shall pay to Composer the sum of . . . and the following royalties . . .

5. Composer represents that he is free to enter into this Agreement . . .

6. Composer agrees to and does hereby grant, bargain, sell and transfer to Producer . . . (rights in music)

7. Composer hereby grants Producer the right to make use of his name . . .

8. Producer may assign this Agreement in its entirety or all or any part of its rights hereunder to any person, firm or corporation.

9. Producer shall have no obligation to produce or complete the production . . .

10. Producer shall have the right to suspend this Agreement . . .

11. Producer shall have the right to edit, rearrange etc. the material composed. Composer hereby waives any so-called "moral rights" of authors.

12. . . . services to be rendered by Composer . . . are of a special, unique, extraordinary and intellectual character . . .

13. All notices or payments which Producer is required or amy desire to give Composer hereunder may be delivered . . . address . . .

14. No waiver by Producer or Composer of any breach . . .

15. Producer may secure insurance on Composer.

16. This agreement shall be governed by and construed under and in accordance with the laws of the State of

California.

17. Composer promises to remain a member in good standing of all applicable unions and guilds.

18. Composer agrees to conduct himself with due regard to public convention, and if he does not, Producer can eliminate Composer's credits.

19. Composer promises to execute future documents necessary to carry out this one.

20. Producer may withhold U.S., state, and union desired monies from wages.

21. Composer acknowledges that no representation or promise not expressly contained in this Agreement has been made by Producer or any of its agents, employees or representatives.

CHAPTER 25

PRODUCER – SCREEN ACTORS GUILD CONTRACT

Producers and individual actors are unequal in bargaining power. Many actors organized the Screen Actors Guild to improve their bargaining power.

Individual actors benefit because their combined power has upped minimum scale, reduced working conditions to writing, and obtained fringe benefits.

Union members suffer because of restrictions placed on them by the union about not working for unapproved and disapproved employers, because of fines, dues, assessments which are or may be payable by the member to the union. Some members pay more in union initiation fees and dues than they ever earn in pictures.

The union member is bound by (1) his contract with the producer, which may be one or two pages and incorporates by reference the provisions of the Producer-SAG Basic Agreement, (2) his contract with the union, including the union constitution and by-laws, (3) the Producer-SAG Codified Basic Agreement.

The producer is bound by above mentioned contracts (1) and (3).

The Producer-SAG Codified Basic Agreement contains General Provisions and separate schedules for Day Players; Free-Lance Players Whose Weekly Guaranteed Salary is $1,500 Or Less Per Week And Who Are Guaranteed Less Than $25,000 Per Picture; Free-Lance Players Whose Weekly Guaranteed Salary Is More Than $1,500 Per Week And Who Are Guaranteed Less Than $25,000 Per Picture; Multiple Picture Players Receiving $1,500 Or Less Per Week And Guaranteed Less Than $25,000 Per Picture; Contract Players Whose Weekly Guaranteed Salary Is $1,500 Or Less Per Week; Contract Players Whose Weekly Guaranteed Salary Is In Excess Of $1,500 Per Week; Multiple Picture Players Receiving More Than $1,500 Per Week Or Who Are Guaranteed $25,00 Or More Per Picture; Players Employed Under "Deal Contracts" Or Otherwise, Who Are Guaranteed $25,000 Or More Per Picture; Professional

Singers Employed By The Day; Professional Singers Employed By The Week At $1,500 Or Less Per Week; Stunt Players Employed By The Day; Stunt Players Employed By The Week At $1,500 Or Less Per Week; Stunt Players Employed By The Week At More Than $1,500 Per Week; Stunt Players Employed Under Term Contracts and Airplane Pilots.

Sample provisions include:

"Every actor hereafter employed by Producer . . . shall be a member of the Guild in good standing."

"Nothing herein contained shall prevent any member of Screen Actors Guild, Inc., from joining and maintaining membership in any union representing extras."

"Producer shall furnish to SAG, written reports showing the gross receipts from the sale, lease, license and distribution of such picture on free television . . ."

" . . . Producer agrees to pay to each actor whose services are included in such motion picture when telecast, compensation not less than the amounts provided herein . . ."

"Pension and Welfare Plan."

"Television Distributors Assumption Agreement."

"Buyer's Assumption Agreement."

"Television Distributor Liability."

"Producer Liability."

"Pay Television."

"Arbitration."

"Disputes Between Guild And Producer."

"Nothing contained in this Agreement shall prevent any individual from negotiating and obtaining from Producer better conditions and terms of employment than those herein contained."

"No part of the photography or sound track of an actor shall be used other than in the picture for which he was employed, without separately bargaining with the actor and reaching an agreement regarding such use."

"Flight Insurance."

"Screen Credits. Producer agrees that a cast of characters on at least one card will be placed at the end of each feature motion picture, naming the actor and the role portrayed."

"Non-Discrimination."

"Tours And Personal Appearances. First class transportation . . . adequate rest periods."

. . . travel allowance . . .

201

"Loan Outs."

"Photography of Legitimate Stage Plays (Instant Movies)."

"Time Cards."

"Pension And Health And Welfare Plans."

"Right To Terminate; Unfair List."

CHAPTER 26

PRODUCER—WRITER CONTRACTS

The Writer who does not belong to the Writers Guild of America West, Inc. or its Eastern brother is free to negotiate with a Producer who has not signed an agreement with the Guild, either.

Once the Guild has the Writer as a member, benefits and burdens are on both parties. Once the Guild has signed with a Producer, benefits and burdens are on both parties.

Writers are free to submit original materials to producers. Producers are not supposed to engage in having the Writer engage in revising such material under continuous direction and supervision by Producer, without the Producer paying the Writer.

The producer and writer generally agree that the services of Writer are of a special, unique, unusual, extraordinary and intellectual character; that the Producer may use Writer's name and reproductions of his physical likeness for advertising and publicity; that the Producer may, but need not, use Writer's creations; that the Writer is an employee-for-hire; that the Writer will conduct himself morally; that while Writer works exclusively for Producer, Writer won't work for anyone else; that Writer's material is original and not stolen; that Writer's material is not defamatory and invades nobody's privacy; that Writer has no authority to spend Producer's money.

The Guild-Producer contract contains many classifications of motion pictures and television films by budget, length of show, steps in writing, and each such classification has a different original and re-run scale.

CHAPTER 27

CLASSROOM EXERCISE

Putting A Picture Together

One of the ways to illustrate the difficulties faced by a producer is to assign roles to students in a class (or members of whatever group is trying to put together a picture).

The roles may be: Businessman-Producer, Creative-Producer, Banker, Completion Bond Company Executiv e, Co-Signer, Laboratory, Director, Male Star, Female Star, Original Writer, Screenplay Writer, Production Manager, Investor, Distributor, Foreign Distributor, TV Rights Buyer, etc.

Each party may have some or all of the following thoughts:

1. To make money for himself.

2. To make money for his employer.

3. To avoid losing money if the film is not produced (the best way to avoid losing money is to spend none).

4. To avoid losing money if the film is produced.

5. To have a maximum personal influence or control over the project while things go right, and even more so, when things go wrong.

The money contributors (investors, lenders), credit contributors (laboratory, deferred income people such as the writer, director, producers, stars), potentially liable parties (co-signers on bank loans, furnishers of the completion bond), potential guarantors (distributor), each would love to have every other person commit himself first.

One day when this play was tried in class, the two co-writers negotiated Contract 1 which provided for a 40-60 split between them, and provided that Writer 1 had full power of attorney to commit Writer 2. (Writer 2 regretted giving that power of attorney to Writer 1.)

Writer 1 assigned the copyright to Creative Producer in exchange for no down payment and a fee payable upon first day of principal photography. (Writer 1 regretted that he had assigned the copyright, and had not given Creative Producer a mere option.)

Creative Producer managed to sign a distribution contract with Distributor and managed to have Distributor promise to contribute $50,000 for post-principal-photography costs (editing, music, additional shooting after the preview). (Creative Producer regretted that he had assigned the copyright in the potential picture to the Distributor when the Banker refused to make the loan because it could not have the copyright as security.)

Producer orally hired one person as Director (both regretted it after a fight; Producer fired Director, Director sued Producer).

In the event the members participating in this exercise should be able to reach oral understandings, the scene may then be thrown into confusion by having the participating members reduce to writing in their own words the agreements they think they reached.

GLOSSARY

The following definitions are for study purposes only. Definitions of a word which may be correct in some states may be incorrect in other states. Definitions of a word applicable under some circumstances may not be applicable under other circumstances.

AGENCY. A fiduciary relationship by which a party confides to another the management of some business to be transacted in the former's name or on his account, and by which such other assumes to do the business and render an account of it.

AGENT. One who acts for and represents the principal, and acquires his authority from him. The agent is a substitute or deputy appointed by the principal with power to do certain things which the principal may or can do.

ARTICLES OF INCORPORATION. The instrument by which a private corporation is formed and organized under general corporation laws.

BYLAWS. The body of rules laid down for the government of a corporation, its officers and stockholders in the conduct of its affairs.

CENSORSHIP. The denial of the right of freedom of speech and of all those rights and privileges which one expects under a free government.

COPYRIGHT. The right of literary property as recognized and sanctioned by positive law. An intangible, incorporeal right granted by statute to the author or originator of certain literary or artistic productions, whereby he is invested, for a limited period, with the sole and exclusive privilege of multiplying copies of the same and publishing and selling them.

CONTRACT. An agreement, upon sufficient consideration, to do or not to do a particular thing.

CORPORATION. A legal entity, existing only in legal contemplation, and is created for the convenience and benefit of the stockholders. A corporation is a creature of the law having certain powers and duties of a natural person.

COURT. A tribunal presided over by one or more judges for the exercise of such judicial power as has been conferred on it by law. A "court" is a place where justice is legally administered.

CRIME. An act committed, or omitted, in violation of a public law forbidding, or commanding it, to which is annexed, upon conviction, one or more of certain specified punishments.

DECREE. The judicial decision of a litigated cause of action by a court.

DEED. A conveyance of realty, a writing signed by grantor, whereby title to realty is transferred from one to another.

DEFAMATION. The taking from one's reputation. The offense of injuring a person's character, fame or reputation by false and malicious statements.

DEFENDANT. The person defending or denying; the party against whom relief or recovery is sought in an action or suit.

EMPLOYEE. The term has no fixed meaning that must control in every instance. In the broadest sense, anyone who performs services for another is an employee pro tempore at least. A hired person who is subject to control of hirer as to means, method and details of performance is "employee" by social security purposes.

EMPLOYER. One who employs. One who uses or engages services of other persons for pay. To constitute a person an employer, he need not actually exercise right of control over employee.

EXPRESS CONTRACT. An actual agreement of the parties, the terms of which are openly uttered or declared at the time of making it, being stated in distinct and explicit language, either orally or in writing.

FEATHERBEDDING. Payment by an employer for services which are not performed or not to be performed. Sometimes employers accuse some movie unions of featherbedding.

FIDUCIARY. A person or organization holding a position and acting in the capacity of trust and special confidence, so that he or it is obliged to act with the highest degree of good faith, and to place ahead of his or its own interests the interest of those represented. Attorneys, guardians, directors of corporations, and public officers are fiduciaries.

FRAUD. An intentional perversion of truth for the purpose of inducing another in reliance upon it to part with some valuable thing belonging to him or to surrender a legal right, a false representation of a matter of fact, whether by words or by conduct, by false or misleading allegations, or by concealment of that which should have been disclosed, which deceives and is intended to deceive another so that he shall act upon it to his legal injury.

FREEDOM OF SPEECH & PRESS. A guarantee, provided by the First and Fourteenth Amendments, against governmental restrictions upon public speeches and publications.

IMPLIED CONTRACT. A contract not created or evidenced by the explicit agreement of the parties, but inferred by the law, as a matter of reason and justice from their acts or conduct, the circumstances surrounding the transaction making it a reasonable, or even a necessary, assumption that a contract existed between them by tacit understanding.

LIBEL. To defame or injure a person's reputation by a published writing. A method of defamation expressed by print, writing, pictures or signs.

LICENSE. Certificate or the document itself which gives permission. Permission or authority. Authority or liberty given to do or forbear any act.

OBSCENE. That to the average person, applying contemporary standards, the predominant appeal to the matter, taken as a whole, is to prurient interest, i.e., a shameful or morbid interest in nudity, sex or excretion, which goes essentially beyond customary limits of candor in description or representation of such matters and is a matter utterly without redeeming social importance.

PARTNERSHIP. An association of two or more persons to carry on as co-owners a business for profit.

PERSONAL PROPERTY. A right or interest, protected by law, in something that is not land or anything permanently attached to land (real property). It may be tangible or intangible.

PLAINTIFF. The party who commences a personal action or suit to obtain a remedy for an alleged injury to his rights.

PLEADINGS. Written statements of the claims and defenses of the parties to a court action.

PRINCIPAL. The party for whom an agent acts and from whom he derives authority to act.

PRIVACY, RIGHT OF. The right to be let alone, the right of a person to be free from unwarranted publicity.

RETRAXIT. An open and voluntary renunciation of his claim by the plaintiff in open court. A "dismissal with prejudice" is the modern name for "retraxit."

SLANDER. A false and unprivileged legal publication, orally uttered, and also communications by radio or any mechanical or other means which (1) charges any person with a crime; (2) imputes in him the present existence of an infectious contagious or loathsome disease; (3) tends directly to injure him in respect to his office, profession, trade or business either by imputing to him general disqualification in those respects whic h the officc or other occupation peculiarly requires, or by imputing something with reference to his office, profession, trade or business that has a natural tendency to lessen its profits; (4) imputes to him impotence or a want of chastity; or (5) which, by natural consequence, causes actual damage.

STOCK (CAPITAL STOCK) Capital of an incorporated company in transferable shares of a specified amount.

STOCKHOLDER. A "holder of record of shares" or a "shareholder of record" and includes a subscriber to shares in cases in which no certificates are outstanding, and a member of a nonstock corporation.

TAX. A charge upon persons or property to raise money for public purposes. It owes its existence to the action of the legislative power, and does not depend for its validity or enforcement upon the individual assent of the taxpayer.

TORT. A violation of a right given or omission of a duty imposed by law. A breach of legal duty. A wrongful act, a private wrong independent of contract and a breach of legal duty.

TORTFEASOR. A person who commits a tort is a "tortfeasor."

TRADEMARK. With reference to registration of trademarks, "trademark" includes every description of word, letter, device, emblem, stamp, imprint, brnad, printed ticket, label, or wrapper, usually affixed by any mechanic, manufacturer, druggist, merchant, or tradesman, to denote any goods to be imported, manufactured, produced, compounded, or sold by him, and also any name or names, marks or devices, branded, stamped, engraved, etched, blown, or otherwise attached or produced upon any cask, cake, bottle, vessel, siphon, can, case, or other package, used by any mechanic, manufacturer, druggist, merchant or tradesman, to hold, contain or inclose the goods so imported, manufactured, produced, compounded or sold by him.

BIBLIOGRAPHY

There are numerous books which you have read or will read concerning lives of stars. These books may be enjoyed by you, as well as by the general public. You, unlike most of the general public, can now pay attention to and better understand the legal aspects of these lives of stars.

AMERICAN FILM INSTITUTE catalog of publications. The John F. Kennedy Center for the Performing Arts. Washington D.C. 20566.
The publications provide information for many persons, including searchers with legal approaches: right of privacy, copyrights, anti-trust, mergers, etc.

BULLETIN OF THE COPYRIGHT SOCIETY OF THE U.S.A. Copyright Society of the U.S.A. New York University Law Center, N.Y., N.Y. 10011.
Articles, Legislative and Administrative Developments, Conventions, Treaties, Proclamations, Judicial Developments, Bibliography.

COPYRIGHT LAW SYMPOSIUM. ASCAP.Columbia University Press, New York.
This annual publication contains prize winning articles by law students on copyright subjects.

ENTERTAINMENT,PUBLISHING AND THE ARTS. Alexander Lindey. Clark Boardman Co. Ltd., New York, N.Y. 10014.
Agreements concerning Books, Magazines, Newspapers, Plays, Motion Pictures, Television, Radio, Music, Phonograph Records, Art Work, Photographs, Merchandising Agencies, etc.

MANAGERS, ENTERTAINERS AND AGENTS BOOK. Johnny Minus and William Storm Hale. 7 Arts Press, Inc., Hollywood, California 90028. $35.00.
Stories, Business Text, Legal Text, Contracts, Forms, etc.

MOVIE BUSINESS, THE William Bluem and Jason E. Squire. Hastings House, New York, N.Y.
Text. Contracts.

MOVIE INDUSTRY BOOK Johnny Minus and William Storm Hale. 7 Arts Press, Inc., Hollywood, Ca. 90028. $35.00.
Especially useful for texts, statutes, cases, contracts, forms.

MUSIC INDUSTRY BOOK, Walter E. Hurst and William Storm Hale. 7 Arts Press, Inc., Hollywood, Ca. 90028. $25.00.
Stories, Business Text, Legal Text, Contracts, Forms, etc.

NIMMER ON COPYRIGHT. Melville B. Nimmer. Matthew Bender, New York, N.Y. 10017.
The currently most popular looseleaf text on copyright.

PERFORMING ARTS REVIEW. The Journal of Management and Law Of The Arts. Entertainment Law Institute of the Law Center, University of Southern California.

PUBLICATIONS OF THE COPYRIGHT OFFICE. Circular 2 Library of Congress. Washington, D.C. 20540. No charge.

PUBLISHERS (music) OFFICE MANUAL Walter E. Hurst and William Storm Hale. 7 Arts Press, Inc., Hollywood, Ca. 90028 $25.00.
Step by Step Guide to Paperwork for a Music Publisher. Simple Flow Charts, Taxes, Contracts, Forms, etc.

RECORD INDUSTRY BOOK. Walter E. Hurst and William Storm Hale. 7 Arts Press, Inc., Hollywood, Ca. 90028. $25.00.
Stories, Business Text, Legal Text, Contracts, Forms, Cartoons, etc.

SEVEN ARTS PRESS, INC. catalog of publications.
6605 Hollywood Boulevard, No. 215, Hollywood, Ca. 90028

THIS BUSINESS OF MUSIC. Sidney Shemel and M. William Krasilovsky. Billboard Publishing Co.
Text and Contracts.

TOTAL FILM-MAKER, THE Jerry Lewis. Random House, New York 1971.
Filmmaking, creative and business aspects.

U.S.MASTER PRODUCERS BOOK. Walter E. Hurst and William Storm Hale. 7 Arts Press, Inc., Hollywood, Ca. 90028. $25.00.
Stories, Business Texts, What to Ask For,Contracts,Forms,etc.

INDEX

MOTION PICTURE AGREEMENT

Agreement made on ⋯⋯⋯⋯⋯⋯⋯⋯⋯⋯⋯⋯⋯
Month   Day   Year

between the United States of America, acting through the Librarian of Congress (herein called the Librarian), and

Name ⋯⋯⋯⋯⋯⋯⋯⋯⋯⋯⋯⋯⋯⋯⋯⋯⋯⋯⋯⋯⋯⋯⋯

Address ⋯⋯⋯⋯⋯⋯⋯⋯⋯⋯⋯⋯⋯⋯⋯⋯⋯⋯⋯⋯⋯⋯
(herein called the Claimant).

WHEREAS:

(a) The undersigned Claimant expects to deposit in the Copyright Office, from time to time, copies of various motion pictures for the registration of its claims to copyright; and

(b) The Librarian is authorized, under section 213 of Title 17, *United States Code*, to select any of such copies for the collections of the Library of Congress (herein called the Library); and

(c) Although for purposes of registration the copyright statute (17 *U.S.C.* §13) requires the deposit of two copies of a published work, in no case is it the policy of the Library to select more than one copyright deposit copy of any motion picture for its collections, and in many cases its acquisitions policies do not provide for the selection or retention of any copy; and

222

(d) Because of the special nature or motion pictures, the forms and modes in which motion pictures are reproduced, distributed, and exhibited can vary widely from case to case and from time to time, and it is to the advantage of both the Claimant and the Library to establish within the framework of the copyright deposit requirements a flexible system for returning, retaining, or recalling deposit copies of motion pictures. The aims of the system are to encourage prompt registration without imposing unnecessary procedural or financial burden on the copyright claimant, and to provide the Library with those copies it wishes to acquire for its collections in the form and condition most suitable for that purpose.

NOW THEREFORE, in consideration of the promises hereinafter set forth, the parties agree as follows:

1. The Claimant shall henceforth, as required by section 13 of Title 17, *United States Code*, and in accordance with the Copyright Office regulations concerning the "best edition" of motion pictures, deposit in the Copyright Office two copies of the "best edition" of every motion picture published with a copyright notice in his name.

2. Promptly after registration the Librarian shall henceforth return to the Claimant, or to an agent designated by him in the application for copyright registration, any and all copies deposited by or for him in connection with every registration for motion pictures published with a copyright notice in his name, with the following exceptions:

(a) In the case of newsreels, television news coverage, and similar motion pictures intended for the contemporaneous reporting of news events, the Librarian shall retain one copy and return one copy; and

(b) In any other case the Librarian may, if requested to do so by the Claimant at the time of copyright registration, retain one copy, in which case he shall return the other copy to the Claimant, or to an agent designated by the Claimant in the application for copyright registration.

223

3. Except in a case where the Librarian has retained a copy under clauses (a) or (b) of paragraph 2, the Claimant shall, during the period of two years after the effective date of copyright registration for a particular motion picture, or until one copy is delivered to the Library in compliance with the written demand of the Librarian under paragraph 5, maintain in his custody or control one good copy, as defined in paragraph 4, of such motion picture, or a negative or master print from which such a good copy can be reproduced.

4. The "good copy" referred to in paragraph 3 shall in all cases be a complete, first quality positive print or fixation of the motion picture that either has not been used for performances or that has been so used that it is substantially clean and undamaged. As a general rule, the "good copy" shall be substantially the same as the two copies of the "best edition" previously deposited for registration in accordance with paragraph 1. The Librarian shall have discretion to accept as the "good copy" a copy different in size, format, or process of reproduction from those deposited.

5. Upon written demand made by the Librarian, or one to whom he has delegated this authority, the Claimant shall deliver to the Library, at the Claimant's expense, one (1) good copy of the motion picture, as defined in paragraph 4. Delivery by the Claimant shall be completed within ninety (90) days after the effective date of demand by the Librarian, or within such additional period of time as the Librarian may stipulate in writing. Said demand shall be made by the Librarian:

(a) when the Claimant, at any time within the two-year period provided by paragraph 3, submits a written request to the Librarian asking that the Library promptly exercise its right to demand delivery of one good copy of the motion picture; in such case, the Librarian shall make said demand not later than ninety (90) days after the receipt of said request; or

(b) within the two-year period provided by paragraph 3, when no request by the Claimant has

6. If, upon delivery of a copy in response to a demand made under paragraph 5, the Librarian determines that it is not a "good copy" as defined in paragraph 4, he shall, within ninety (90) days of said delivery, make an additional written demand for the delivery of one good copy in substitution for the delivered copy, and the Claimant shall have ninety (90) days, or such additional period of time as the Librarian may stipulate in writing, in which to deliver said substituted copy. If a substitute copy is received and accepted, the copy delivered earlier will be returned to the Claimant.

7. If the Claimant fails to deliver the good copy of a motion picture within the periods provided by or stipulated under paragraphs 5 or 6, and if it shall be established that thereby the Claimant has breached this agreement with respect to that motion picture, the Librarian shall have the right to acquire one good copy or the right to reproduce one good copy, and the Claimant shall be liable for the full costs of such acquisition or reproduction.

8. In cases where the Librarian has made no demand within the periods of time provided by paragraphs 5 or 6, the Claimant shall cease to have any obligation under this agreement with respect to the particular motion picture at the end of such periods.

9. As part of his obligations under this Agreement, the Librarian shall not cause, authorize, or permit, without the prior written consent of the copyright owner:

(a) any public performance of copyrighted motion pictures, or any private performance of such motion pictures other than for research or study purposes, or any use or performance outside the premises of the Library, with the use of prints or fixations in the Library collections; or

(b) any exchange, transfer, sale, or gift, to another library or any other recipient, or the making of any copy of any deposited copy of a motion picture retained under clauses (a) or (b), paragraph 2, or delivered in response to a demand or without a demand under paragraphs 5 or 6 or acquired or reproduced under paragraph 7.

10. Either party may terminate this Agreement for good cause upon thirty (30) days written notice to the other party. Such termination shall apply only to motion pictures of which copies are thereafter deposited by the Claimant, and shall not affect the rights of the Librarian or the obligations of either party with respect to any motion pictures of which copies have been returned under paragraph 2, or have been deposited or reproduced pursuant to Paragraphs 5, 6, or 7.

11. The Claimant may assign this Agreement insofar as it applies to copies of motion pictures deposited for copyright registration after written notice of the assignment to the Librarian. Such notice shall be accompanied by a copy or duplicate original of the assignment.

12. No assignment of this Agreement shall, without the written consent of the other party, relieve either party of the rights and obligations previously assumed and subsisting with respect to copies of motion pictures deposited before receipt by the Librarian of the written notice specified by paragraph 11. However, all rights and obligations under this agreement whether previously assumed and subsisting or arising in the future, shall bind and inure to the benefit of the executors, administrators, legal representatives, heirs, or distributees of the Claimant in cases where title to such rights and obligations has been transferred by operation of law.

13. All notices required hereunder shall be written and shall be directed to the respective parties at the addresses set forth above except as the same may from time to time be changed in writing. In the event that the undersigned claimant changes the address of his place of business, or the address to which notices under this agreement are to be delivered, he shall promptly notify the Exchange and Gift Division of the Library of such change in address.

14. Regardless of the place of its physical execution, this Agreement shall be interpreted according to the laws and statutes of the United States of America, and of the District of Columbia.

15. In the case of any motion picture having two or more copyright claimants, this Agreement shall be binding if any of the persons listed as a copyright claimant in the notice of copyright appearing on the copies or in the application for copyright registration is a signatory to this or another copy of the present Agreement, and **(such signatory or signatories) shall be responsible, jointly or severally**, with respect to the delivery of a good copy of that motion picture.

16. This Agreement constitutes the complete understanding of the parties. No modification or waiver of any provision hereof shall be valid unless in writing and signed by both parties.

IN WITNESS WHEREOF the parties have duly executed this Agreement.

THE UNITED STATES OF AMERICA

by ....
Librarian of Congress

BOND TO BE SIGNED BY ATTORNEY-IN-FACT

Know All Men by these Presents, that I, ... , having signed,

of . . . .
Address

as attorney-in-fact for Claimant, the Motion Picture Agreement between the United States of America,

acting through the Librarian of Congress, and . . . .
Claimant

executed on . . . . , am held and firmly bound
Date

unto the United States of America as follows:

The condition of this obligation is such that if the Claimant named above, or his executors, administrators, legal representatives, heirs or assigns shall in all things well and truly perform and observe all the
covenants, agreements, and conditions on his or their part to be performed and observed with respect to a
given motion picture which are contained in the Agreement made and bearing even date herewith, then this
obligation shall be void with respect to that motion picture; otherwise to remain in full force.

I am bound in a penal sum representing the full cost of acquiring or of reproducing one good copy of
any motion picture registered by the Copyright Office under the terms of the above Agreement, but in no
case shall this sum be less than two hundred dollars ($200.00) per film.

By . . . .
Attorney-in-fact

228

Public Law 92-140
92nd Congress, S. 646
October 15, 1971

An Act

To amend title 17 of the United States Code to provide for the creation of a limited copyright in sound recordings for the purpose of protecting against unauthorized duplication and piracy of sound recording, and for other purposes.

Be it enacted by the Senate and House of Representatives of the United States of America in Congress assembled, That title 17 of the United States Code is amended in the following respects:

Sound recordings.
Copyright.
Limitations.
61 Stat. 652;
66 Stat. 752.

(a) In section 1, title 17, of the United States Code, add a subsection (f) to read:

"To reproduce and distribute to the public by sale or other transfer of ownership, or by rental, lease, or lending, reproductions of the copyrighted work if it be a sound recording: *Provided,* That the exclusive right of the owner of a copyright in a sound recording to reproduce it is limited to the right to duplicate the sound recording in a tangible form that directly or indirectly recaptures the actual sounds fixed in the recording: *Provided further.* That this right does not extend to the making or duplication of another sound recording that is an independent fixation of other sounds, even though such sounds imitate or simulate those in the copyrighted sound recording; or to reproductions made by transmitting organizations exclusively for their own use."

(b) In section 5, title 17, of the United States Code, add a subsection (n) to read:

"Sound recordings."

(c) In section 19, title 17, of the United States Code, add the following at the end of the section: "In the case of reproductions of works specified in subsection (n) of section 5 of this title, the notice shall consist of the symbol ℗ (the letter P in a circle), the year of first publication of the sound recording, and the name of the owner of copyright in the sound recording, or an abbreviation by which the name can be recognized, or a generally known alternative designation of the owner: *Provided,* That if the producer of the sound recording is named on the labels or containers of the reproduction, and if no other name appears in conjunction with the notice, his name shall be considered a part of the notice."

Copyright notice, form.
68 Stat. 1032.

(d) In section 20, title 17, of the United States Code, amend the first sentence to read: "The notice of copyright shall be applied, in the case of a book or other printed publication, upon its title page or the page immediately following, or if a periodical either upon the title page or upon the first page of text of each separate number or under the title heading, or if a musical work either upon its title page or the first page of music, or if a sound recording on the surface of reproductions thereof or on the label or container in such manner and location as to give reasonable notice of the claim of copyright."

Notice, location.

(e) In section 26, title 17, of the United States Code, add the following at the end of the section: "For the purposes of this section and sections 10, 11, 13, 14, 21, 101, 106, 109, 209, 215, but not for any other purpose, a reproduction of a work described in subsection 5(n) shall be considered to be a copy thereof. 'Sound recordings' are works that result from the fixation of a series of musical, spoken, or other sounds, but not including the sounds accompanying a motion picture. 'Reproductions of sound recordings' are material objects in which sounds other than those accompanying a motion picture are fixed by any method now known or later developed, and from which the sounds can be perceived, reproduced, or otherwise communicated, either directly or with the aid of a machine or device, and include the 'parts

Definitions.

Supra.

229

85 STAT. 392

of instruments serving to reproduce mechanically the musical wor 'mechanical reproductions', and 'interchangeable parts, such as di or tapes for use in mechanical music-producing machines' referred in sections 1(e) and 101(e) of this title."

61 Stat. 652.
17 USC 1.
Infra.
Copyrighted
music, un-
authorized
use.
61 Stat. 661.

SEC. 2. That title 17 of the United States Code is further amend in the following respect:

In section 101, title 17 of the United States Code, delete subsecti (e) in its entirety and substitute the following:

"(e) INTERCHANGEABLE PARTS FOR USE IN MECHANICAL MUS PRODUCING MACHINES.—Interchangeable parts, such as discs or tap for use in mechanical music-producing machines adapted to reprodu copyrighted musical works, shall be considered copies of the cop righted musical works which they serve to reproduce mechanically f the purposes of this section 101 and sections 106 and 109 of this tit and the unauthorized manufacture, use, or sale of such interchang able parts shall constitute an infringement of the copyrighted wo rendering the infringer liable in accordance with all provisions of t title dealing with infringements of copyright and, in a case of willf infringement for profit, to criminal prosecution pursuant to secti

Notice.

104 of this title. Whenever any person, in the absence of a licen agreement, intends to use a copyrighted musical composition upon t parts of instruments serving to reproduce mechanically the music work, relying upon the compulsory license provision of this title, shall serve notice of such intention, by registered mail, upon the cop right proprietor at his last address disclosed by the records of t copyright office, sending to the copyright office a duplicate of su notice."

Effective dates.

SEC. 3. This Act shall take effect four months after its enactme except that section 2 of this Act shall take effect immediately upon : enactment. The provisions of title 17, United States Code, as amend by section 1 of this Act, shall apply only to sound recordings fixe published, and copyrighted on and after the effective date of this A and before January 1, 1975, and nothing in title 17, United Stat Code, as amended by section 1 of this Act, shall be applied retr actively or be construed as affecting in any way any rights with respe to sound recordings fixed before the effective date of this Act.

Approved October 15, 1971.

LEGISLATIVE HISTORY:

HOUSE REPORT No. 92-487 (Comm. on the Judiciary).
SENATE REPORT No. 92-72 (Comm. on the Judiciary).
CONGRESSIONAL RECORD, Vol. 117, (1971):
    Apr. 29, considered and passed Senate.
    Oct. 4, considered and passed House, amended.
    Oct. 6, Senate agreed to House amendments.

WHAT FILM STUDENTS STATED
ABOUT STUDYING LAW

"I feel that this class has been worth my time and effort. It has given me an insight to some of the pitfalls I can come up against when I enter the film industry."

"I want to be a law abiding and successful person, so I must learn the laws."

"I heard about a film being stopped in mid-production by police. I now understand more about legal and illegal obscenity."

"What I especially liked was being informed where I can obtain even more information."

"I am almost discouraged enough by legal complexities to not go into motion pictures. But, I suppose everything has legal complexities so I will go into motion pictures."

"I know that I am going to read every contract carefully. I am not just going to leave the reading of my contracts to my lawyer. Only with both of us reading contracts and making changes, will I have a chance to make lots of money."

"How do so many people get away with so much so often? And, how can I? I would love to know."

"No wonder talented people come and go, but law knowledge-able people grow and grow."

THE MOVIE INDUSTRY BOOK
by Johnny Minus and William Storm Hale
7 Arts Press — $35.00
6605 Hollywood Boulevard No. 215
Hollywood, California 90028

PARTS:

This book is ideal for the show business producer, attorney and wondering potential investor.

FLASH

We are used to receiving news only a few hours after the event (TV), a day after the event (newspapers), a week after the event (news magazines).

You can reasonably expect news (new statutes, decisions, Copyright Office forms and circulars) to occur.

In 1972 Congress passed a new law protecting sound recordings (ask the Copyright Office for Circular 56 and Form N); and in 1972 Congress extended protection for works now being protected under the renewal or extension provisions of the Copyright Law until December 31, 1972. Congress will keep on trying, and sometimes succeeding to pass more copyright laws.

During the interval between the writing and your reading this book, other changes may have occurred. (Statutes, Court Decisions, Treaties.)

Nobody is perfect. That includes US — We may have put misinformation in this book. That includes you — you may not be interpreting correctly sentences or other parts of this book.

Naturally, we advise you to see qualified attorneys qualified in the specialty in which you are interested, when you need legal advice.

Having mentioned all the above, we want to be very positive.

This book is terrific. It is fact filled, law filled, informative and readable.

For fun and profit it is an excellent introduction to a sought field.

For more humor, see inside.